Map from New International Atlas
© 1992 by Rand McNally, R.L. 92-S-85

Map from Goode's World Atlas
© 1992 by Rand McNally, R.L. 92-S-85

Enchantment of the World

SAUDI ARABIA

By Leila Merrell Foster

Consultant for Saudi Arabia: Sandra D. Batmangelich, M.A., Outreach Director, Center for Middle Eastern Studies, The University of Chicago, Chicago, Illinois

Consultant for Reading: Robert L. Hillerich, Ph.D., Visiting Professor, University of South Florida; Consultant, Pinellas County Schools, Florida

CHILDRENS PRESS®
CHICAGO

Saudi Arabian children

Project Editor: Mary Reidy
Design: Margrit Fiddle

Library of Congress Cataloging-in-Publication Data

Foster, Leila Merrell.
    Saudi Arabia / by Leila Merrell Foster.
        p.   cm. — (Enchantment of the world)
    Includes index.
    Summary: Describes the history, geography, culture,
industry, and economy of the largest country on the
Arabian Peninsula.
    ISBN 0-516-02611-9
    1.   Saudi Arabia—Juvenile literature.   [1.   Saudi
Arabia.]   I.   Title.   II.   Series.
DS204.F74   1993   92-8890
953.8—dc20   CIP
                                                                      AC

Picture Acknowledgments
AP/Wide World Photos: 55, 59, 60 (right), 61 (2 photos),
62, 71 (2 photos)
The Bettmann Archive: 36, 49, 53
H. Armstrong Roberts: © **K. Scholz,** 14 (left), 74 (left)
Historical Pictures: 35
Photri: 6, 24 (2 photos), 25 (left), 76; © **Mehmet Biber,** 14
(right), 18 (2 photos), 27 (right), 28 (left), 67, 68 (right), 72
(top left), 74 (right), 79, 84 (left), 85, 86 (left), 87 (left), 90,
98, 101, 102 (bottom right)

© **Carl Purcell:** 16 (right)
© **Reynolds Photography:** 15 (right)
Root Resources: © **Ian C. Tait,** 12 (center), 33
Courtesy of Saudi Arabian Information Office,
Washington, D.C.: 39, 81, 82, 89 (right), 120, 121
Tom Stack & Associates: © **Bryon Augustin,** 11, 13
(right), 23, 44 (top), 69, 72 (top right and bottom right), 73,
86 (right), 87 (right), 93, 102 (bottom left); © **John Shaw,**
15 (center); © **Gary Milburn,** 16 (center)
SuperStock International, Inc.: 15 (left); © **Hubertus**
Kanus, Cover; © **Peter Schmid,** Cover Inset, 25 (right);
© **Leonard Lee Rue III,** 12 (right); © **Kurt Scholz,** 12 (left);
© **The Photo Source,** 75 (right); © **Robert Abrams,** 29, 75
(left)
TSW-CLICK/Chicago: © **Don Smetzer,** 4, 21, 22, 30, 31
(2 photos), 40, 44 (bottom), 68 (left), 83, 84 (right); © **Jane**
Lewis, 5, 8, 9, 13 (left), 27 (left), 28 (top and bottom right),
89 (left), 102 (top left and right), 103, 106; © **Peter**
Carmichael, 72 (bottom left); © **David Austen,** 80;
© **Nabeel Turner,** 92, 96, 97
UPI/Bettmann Newsphotos: 51 (2 photos), 56, 57
(2 photos), 60 (left)
Valan: © **Kennon Cooke,** 16 (left), 17 (left); © **Paul L.**
Janosi, 17 (inset)
Len W. Meents: Maps on 21, 25, 27, 30
Courtesy Flag Research Center, Winchester,
Massachusetts 01890: Flag on back cover
Cover: National Commercial Bank, Jiddah
Cover Inset: Market, Jiddah

A Najdi craftsman at work

TABLE OF CONTENTS

A photo taken 340 miles (547 kilometers) above the earth shows the Arabian Peninsula on the top separated from Africa by the Red Sea and the Gulf of Aden. The rose-colored area in the top center shows Rub' al-Khali, the largest continuous expanse of sand desert in the world.

Chapter 1

SAND-COVERED
OIL FIELDS

At the western side of Asia not far from the continent of Africa lies Saudi Arabia, the largest country on the Arabian Peninsula. Saudi Arabia is a country where great deserts cover vast oil reserves, where Muslim pilgrims come to the Holy Cities of Mecca (sometimes spelled Makkah) and Medina, and where the Arab peoples began their movement to other countries.

The Arabian Peninsula is surrounded on three sides by sea: to the east, the Persian or Arabian Gulf and the Gulf of Oman; to the south, the Arabian Sea, and to the west, the Red Sea. At the northern end are deserts.

Several smaller countries also are located on the Arabian Peninsula. Kuwait is in the north. To the east are the nations of Bahrain (islands in the Persian Gulf), Qatar, the United Arab Emirates, and Oman. To the south is Yemen.

With its 830,000 square miles (2,149,690 square kilometers), Saudi Arabia is larger than Alaska or Mexico. With a population of more than fifteen million, it has fewer people than the state of New York.

FORMATION OF THE LAND

After an upheaval that took place geological ages ago, the Arabian Peninsula was formed. According to a theory about the

The southwest area is mountainous.

formation of the continents, plates on which landmasses are
located were split apart as currents of molten rock pushed up
from inside the earth. The Arabian Peninsula that was once a part
of the African continent was pushed north. The western edge was
higher and so, as the rock weathered, new layers of land were
deposited on the lower land to the east. As the Red Sea pushed in
between Africa and Saudi Arabia, molten rock called lava welled
up in the west. In some places it covered the old layers. The lava
flowed out and solidified to form great fields of this crusted rock.

Along the Red Sea there is a narrow coastal plain. South of
Mecca are the highest peaks in Saudi Arabia—some over 8,200 feet
(2,499 meters). East of the highland area are plateaus and basins
where subsurface water collects, allowing humans to live in cities
such as Medina and Khaybar. Still farther east, at lower altitudes,
are sedimentary rocks such as soft sandstone and harder
limestone. Valleys form in the soft layers, while limestone pokes
up into ridges. One of these limestone ridges, *Jabal Tuwayq*

Red sands of the desert

(Tuwayq escarpment), is 3,200 feet (975 meters) high and lies to the west of Riyadh, the capital and one of the fastest-growing cities in the Middle East. Riyadh is located in a gap that breaks through the great ridge.

Another of these ridges occurs farther east, near Hufuf. Here the land level drops to form the low coastal plain along the Persian Gulf. Some of the lowlands are bare rock, but most are covered by loose stone that has been eroded by wind, shattered by temperature contrasts, or broken up by water. Gravel, sand, and silt are found here.

In the north, a large expanse of sand dunes is located in the interior. It is called *an-Nafud*, "the Great Nafud." The sand is often a reddish color and there are areas of bare rock. A narrow zone of sand, Dahna', lies between the Nafud and the Rub' al-Khali in the south, the largest continuous expanse of sand desert in the world. *Rub' al-Khali* can be translated "Empty Quarter." In the southeast this desert is a sea of sand with gravel plains around it; and in the east are dunes with salt basins. It is not a place where people would usually choose to live. However, the discovery of oil and artesian water under some of this surface is likely to bring people into the territory to develop these natural resources.

ONE OF THE DRIEST COUNTRIES

The air masses that come to Arabia from the north and west have had most of their moisture squeezed out after passage over other lands. As a result, Saudi Arabia is very dry. It has a long, hot, dry summer and a short, cool winter when a little rain falls. With the lack of clouds, summer temperatures shoot up to 111 degrees to 122 degrees Fahrenheit (44 degrees to 50 degrees Celsius)—and even higher in the south. The lack of cloud cover also permits the heat to escape at night so that night temperatures drop rapidly. Sometimes there is even frost in the interior and the north. Riyadh has recorded a low of 19 degrees Fahrenheit (minus 7 degrees Celsius).

What rainfall does occur comes mostly between the months of October and April. Some areas may not get any rain for as long as ten years. When rain does come, it can be a "gully washer," dropping as much as six inches (fifteen centimeters) in a twenty-four-hour period.

The temperature contrasts produce strong winds. In midwinter and early summer, a wind carrying dust and sand can blow from the north. It is called *shamal*, meaning "north." A less frequent wind called *kaus* comes from the southeast. In the desert areas, the wind flow is more complicated and can come from any direction with varying intensities. Along the coast, the sea breezes bring high humidity. Here fog and dew can be a substitute for rain.

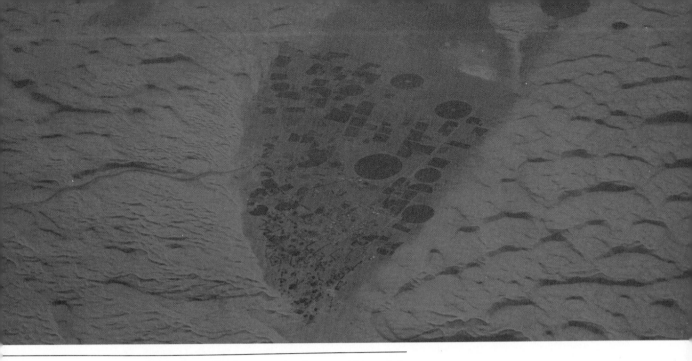

An aerial view of a desert oasis shows uniform plots of land that have been irrigated and cultivated.

When rain does fall, it can fill watercourses called *wadis*. A wadi may contain a torrent of water when it is raining, although it is dry most of the year. Without any year-round rivers or lakes, the underground water tapped by wells can be of vital importance.

Because of the dry climate and lack of good soil, the country originally could support only a small population. As many as one-fourth of the people—the Bedouin—adopted a nomadic life-style, moving themselves and their herds of animals to and from *oases*, areas where natural springs or wells supply water. However, with the money from oil fields, it has been possible for the country to plan irrigation and to locate underground water supplies. Now the population has increased four or five times. Cities have grown.

PLANTS OF SAUDI ARABIA

The date palm is an important plant and is found where there is enough water, except at very high elevations. Dates are an

Dates (inset above left) are grown on date palm plantations (above). The pomegranate (inset right) is one of the popular fruits grown in Saudi Arabia.

important element of the diet of both city and desert dwellers. The trunk, branches, and fiber of the palm are used. Dates from the regions of Madinah and Bishah oasis are noted for quality. Alfalfa, used for fodder for animals, may be grown among the palms.

Wheat, barley, and millet are the primary grain crops. Small patches of these grain crops may be planted in moist wadi beds out in the desert areas. Rice is a popular food item, but little of it is grown locally. Cotton is produced in a few places.

Fruit is prized more than vegetables. Grapes, melons, pomegranates, jujubes, mangoes, figs, bananas, and prickly pears are favored. Citrons and java almonds are raised in the oases.

Coffee is cultivated on the mountain terraces of the Asir region. A shrub that produces a narcotic called *kat* can be grown in the coffee areas and is profitable for the grower.

Mimosa and acacia plants are found in Asir but are not utilized much on a commercial basis. Plants that produce dyes such as

The King's Park near Ta'if (above) and roses under cultivation in a desert greenhouse (inset left)

indigo are grown, and the dyes are used on cloth and in decorating the human body. It is stylish to trace designs on the hands for special occasions.

Flowers are rare, but the roses of Ta'if are famous. The oleander lives even in the desert and provides accents of color to an otherwise bland setting. Annuals that bloom with the winter rains include the desert antheimis, mustard plants, and a type of iris.

Trees are so rare that the Arabic word for tree is also used for bushes that provide firewood and grazing for animals. Junipers can be found in the southwestern highlands. The tamarisk, which can live in the dry climate, is sometimes planted in rows to retard the drifting sand. Twigs from the *rak* shrub are used as toothbrushes. Camels find enough salt in the leaves of the *hadh*, a prickly bush, to keep healthy. When the rains do come, the truffle grows and is dug out of the ground by the Bedouin.

13

Before modern transportation, the only way to travel was by camel (left). Now even the camel can sometimes enjoy a ride.

SHIPS OF THE DESERT AND OTHER ANIMALS

Living in a sea of sand required the "ship of the desert," the camel. Before trucks, cars, railroads, and airplanes, about the only way to get around in a country like Saudi Arabia was by riding a camel. Camels are still used by some of the people of Saudi Arabia. Not only does the camel supply humans with a form of transportation, but it gives milk that sustains travelers between wells of water. Its flesh provides meat; its hair, clothing; its dung, fuel for fires.

The shape of the camel's large foot helps to prevent the animal from sinking into the sand. When the rider comes to a well, the rope to the bucket can be attached to the camel so that the animal helps draw up the water. The camel also can be used for plowing. Obviously this animal is a valuable asset to own or to trade.

Camels are still used, but much less today than in earlier times. The Bedouins also use modern transportation methods. Cars,

*An Arabian horse (left), an ibex (center),
and a saluki (right)*

trucks, buses, trains, and planes transport people and goods
throughout the region.

Sheep are kept for their meat and wool; goats, for goat cheese.
Dairy cattle have been introduced to the country. The famous
Arabian horse is disappearing from Arabia, though it is bred in
other countries, where it is prized for its beauty and stamina.
Large white donkeys, humped and regular cows, and chickens are
raised in some parts of the country.

People hunt with a breed of dog called a saluki, famed for its
speed. The training of falcons to use in hunting is an important
activity. In less than three weeks the most skilled falconers can
train a falcon to hunt other birds.

Gazelles, oryx, and ibex are prey that have been hunted to the
point of becoming rare. The oryx, when seen in profile from a
distance, looks as though it has a single horn. It may have given
rise to the legends of the unicorn. Zoos such as the one in San
Diego, California, have been helping to introduce oryx born in

The Arabian oryx (left) and the sand cat (center) are rarely seen. Baboons (right) live in the southern mountains.

captivity back into their Arabian habitat. The Saudi government is interested in conservation and restocking efforts.

The lion is extinct here, but hyenas and wolves can be found. Numbers of baboons live in the southern mountains, where they raid terraced croplands. The smaller animals include the fox, ratel, rabbit, hedgehog, and gerbil. A rare sand cat that looks like a domestic cat has found a way to live in some of the most desolate areas.

The desert is also home to some snakes; over a dozen species live there, but are seldom seen. The sand viper, venomous but not deadly, and various types of cobras live in the desert. The seas harbor poisonous, but shy, sea snakes. Monitor lizards and skinks are found in the desert also.

Among the birds, ostriches, once found in Saudi Arabia, are extinct; but eagles, vultures, owls, and the lesser bustard are

Flamingos (above) live along the coast, and groupers (inset) live in the sea.

common. The coastal areas are home to flamingos, egrets, and other seabirds. Smaller birds such as swallows and cuckoos can be found around settled areas. Sand grouse and larks inhabit desert regions.

Food from the sea includes mackerel, groupers, tuna, porgies, shrimp, and sardines. Sharks are numerous off the southern coast of the peninsula, and an occasional whale swims into the Persian Gulf.

Locusts can be especially destructive when they swarm in numbers. They eat almost any growing plant in sight. Locusts, in turn, are considered a delicacy and are used in the Saudi diet. Flies, mosquitoes, ticks, beetles, scorpions, and ants can add to the level of human discomfort. In some places, bees are kept for honey production.

Above: Sheep near a watering area in the mountains
Below: Twisting roads have been built through the mountains and highlands.

Chapter 2

TOWN AND DESERT PEOPLE

Although much of Saudi Arabia is desert land, towns always have been important as trading and cultural centers. Life in these centers has differed from the life of the Bedouin, who needed to move from place to place to sustain life for themselves and their animals. While the townspeople and the Bedouin depended on each other, their different life-styles created a certain degree of tension. For the Bedouin, the allegiance to the tribal family was essential for survival. For the town dweller, the family was still of great importance, but the city provided more opportunities for individual initiative.

Still, there are many characteristics that these two groups in Saudi Arabia have in common. Arabic is the language they speak. With its Holy Cities of Mecca and Medina, the country is considered the center of the Islamic religion. About 85 percent of the Saudi Muslims are Sunnis, and the remainder are Shi'ites.

The country can be divided into four districts: Central, Western, Southwest, and Eastern.

CENTRAL

The people living in this area are known as the Najdis. *Najd* means "highland." It is an area that has been somewhat isolated by the mountain barrier of the Hijaz to the west and sand barriers on the other sides. The people are known for their conservatism. They dress in traditional clothing—long robes and headdresses—that has been worn for centuries.

While fighting with outsiders was rare because few persons were attracted to invade this territory, bickering between tribes, between towns, and between tribe and town was frequent. Yet the area is known for the Arab traditions of hospitality and generosity that are so important to travelers in such barren territory. A stranded traveler is treated as one of the family. Sharing food, a cool drink, and a cup of coffee with another is natural for an Arab, and it is considered an insult to decline.

Religious issues have been important factors in the history of this territory. As the Islamic religion spread from Mecca and Medina, it encountered resistance in central Najd where a prophet was teaching a creed considered false by the early leaders of Islam. A famous general, Khalid ibn al-Walid, known as the "Sword of God (Allah)," was dispatched to see that the true faith was taught. Once the Najdis were convinced, they equipped many warriors and missionaries to spread the faith to others.

In the eighteenth century, another significant religious event was the alliance of a scholar of this area, Sheikh Muhammad ibn Abd al-Wahhab, with the ruler of the oasis of Diriyah, Muhammad ibn Saud. This scholar started the Wahhabi movement, designed to return Islam to the original teaching and form found in the revelations to Muhammad, the Prophet of Islam. Muhammad ibn Saud was to extend his power over all of Saudi Arabia.

In the twentieth century, this alliance was tested. The ruler, the late King Abd al-Aziz, known as Ibn Saud, had to determine what new inventions should be let into the country. He took the

A section of the capital city of Riyadh

position that modern conveniences such as the automobile and the telephone were useful to the community and not harmful to religious beliefs. Some of the tribal chiefs from the Najd rejected this position. The chiefs also wanted to be able to conduct raids on Arabs in neighboring states that they considered to be infidels or unbelievers. Ibn Saud placed restraints on such raids. The chiefs revolted but were crushed by Ibn Saud with the help of some of the townspeople of the Najd.

Riyadh, the capital of the country, is in this area. When this great city with its many new buildings is viewed today, it is difficult to realize that in the 1940s this settlement was a walled town built with mud bricks. Only a few roads were paved, and construction of airports was just beginning. Formal education was possible only in religion and the Arabic language. Now the money from oil has produced a great city. Primary and secondary schools are available for everyone. Riyadh has universities for both men and women.

A typical Saudi meal features lamb served on a bed of rice. Fruit is eaten as part of the dessert.

Though young Najdis take advantage of these modern opportunities, they also prize traditional values. There is still a deep love of the desert. The sword dance is honored. Time is made for conversation accompanied by the traditional coffee and sweet tea. Banquets are served on rugs. Lamb served on a bed of seasoned rice is a popular dish. A poet recites his verse. The last course of the banquet is a sweet dessert. Then the incense burner is passed around signaling the time for guests to leave.

WESTERN

This area contains the territory to which devout Muslims have come over the centuries to fulfill their obligation to visit the Holy Cities of Mecca and Medina. Camel caravans overland and ships on the sea brought the pilgrims to this land before railroads and airports were built.

In the north where it is arid, a large population cannot be supported. Where there is water, small communities have taken

The Hijaz *refers to the "barrier" that separates the towns along the coast from the interior plateau.*

advantage of the resource. Medina has been able to support a larger population because at Medina water flows from beneath a huge lava field. South of the towns of Jiddah and Ta'if, regular rains support hundreds of small farming villages.

Part of this territory is called the *Hijaz*, which means "barrier," referring to the escarpment or high ridge that runs along its length and separates it from the interior plateau. This barrier defined the trade routes along which products traveled to the markets in the rest of the world. Mecca, Medina, Khubar, Tayma', and Tabuk were towns that developed as stopping points and trading centers where caravans could rest and get water supplies.

Even before Islamic times, the city of Mecca was a pilgrimage and cultural center. Since Mecca became the center of the Islamic world, many different people have come. Some have decided to stay. In the south along the coast are settlements where people of African descent live in thatch houses. The highlands are where people of a Semitic background live.

Desalination of the seawater has allowed the city of Jiddah (above) to provide water for its citizens and to grow trees. Workers on a pier at Jiddah's port (right)

In the rural and village areas, family relationships are of great importance and can be recited from memory in detail. In the cities, while the traditional families still are honored, they are in competition with business, technical, and professional people from outside.

Experts connected with the major oil companies from the United States and Great Britain have helped the growth of the petroleum industry. The industrialization that has been supported by oil money has attracted workers from Syria, Palestine, Egypt, Pakistan, Lebanon, and Iraq. For the most part, these persons have settled in the cities. Women seeking domestic jobs have come from

A highway (above) has been built to connect the city of Jiddah with Ta'if (inset).

Ethiopia, Somalia, and the Philippines. The nomads of the area have tended to settle on the outskirts of towns and cities, giving up their tents for houses and their camels for trucks.

The cities have growing populations. Jiddah is a commercial and industrial center. Improvements have been made to handle the great influx of pilgrims at Mecca. Medina is the center of the Islamic universities, with colleges of basic religion, religious law, and missions. Ta'if at its high elevation has become the second capital in the summer, when people go there to escape the summer heat. Ta'if also is known as a supplier of fruit for the area and for its rosewater (*attar*) that is made from the acres of roses grown there.

SOUTHWEST

The traditional name for this area is *Asir*, "the difficult region," probably referring to the difficulty for the traveler. The peaks and valleys made the route to the south hazardous before the building of highways. Because the mountains rise up from the coastal plain, the area was not easy to approach from the west. Toward the east, the slope is gentler but leads to the great sand desert. Deep valleys and rugged hills form the border with Yemen.

This territory gets a good amount of rain. Much of the rain comes with the summer *monsoons* (seasonal rains) when rain falls in torrents. Over the centuries, farmers have developed walled step terraces to keep the soil from washing away. Cereals, fodder, and fruit are grown in this area. To protect their houses from the weather, the people have mortared rows of louvers into the outer walls. The outside walls of the homes are painted in bright colors.

Bright colors also are favored by the women for their clothing. Metal jewelry with intricate designs is worn.

There are differences between the highland and the lowland people of the region. Highlanders tend to be somewhat taller. In the highlands, the villagers build their houses in different styles. Before this area was incorporated into Saudi Arabia a few generations ago, there was a great deal of feuding between villages. The many watchtowers in the countryside are evidence from the past of this fighting.

Today, the area suitable for cultivation of crops is being extended by irrigation. Marketing and transportation of agricultural products are provided. Many of the farmers own cars, trucks, and agricultural machinery. Schools, hospitals, roads, and dams have been introduced to the region.

Riyadh ✦

Najran ·

Above: At the oasis of Najran, the buildings have thick mud-brick walls and the roofs are wooden beams that are covered with straw and then with mud. Left: The ghutrah, the red-and-white checkered cloth worn on the head by Saudi Arabian men, is a very common sight.

At the southern end of this area is the oasis of Najran. The language used here links the area with the Najd. Its location and the mud-and-straw buildings identify it with the southwest. The half-moon-shaped windows are of tinted glass. Situated in the sand desert, Najran is frequently visited by Bedouin. Dates and grapes are the chief products of this oasis.

The clothing of the men, like that of the Najdis, is a long robe called a *thawb*. Here the color may be white, blue, or olive. A *ghutrah*, a red-and-white checkered cloth, is worn on the head and held in place by an *agal*, a black or white cord. The women, unlike the Nadjis, wear *abhas*, long-waisted, bright-colored dresses with embroidery. They do not wear veils. Women who work in the fields wear broad-brimmed hats similar to a sombrero.

In the Tihamah area is the village of Rijal. Stone houses rise up

*Above: Rainwater stored in the Jizan Dam
has helped change the surrounding land into
an area where grain is grown. A Bedouin tent (top right)
and a curved dagger (right) that some Bedouin carry*

the side of the steep slopes of the narrow valley. Inside the houses
are stylized designs painted on the walls by the women. Also
adding color are imported enamelware items on the shelves. The
village is famous for its goldsmithing.

Rijal is home to farmers who raise the usual crops at the bottom
of the valley and coffee at the higher elevations. Nomads raising
sheep and goats also inhabit the area. These Bedouin dress quite
differently. The men are bare chested and wear a colorful cloth
wrapped around the lower part of their bodies. A curved dagger is
their protection against leopards, which are rare. A tall brimless
black hat completes their outfit. The women wear tall straw hats
with brims.

The coastal area of Tihamah is flat and sandy. The farmers grow
mostly millet. Thanks to the Jizan Dam that stores some of the
rainwater, new land has been brought under cultivation. The
government runs an experimental farm in the area.

The Red Sea coast

To the south along the Red Sea, fishing is an important industry. Much of the fishing is done at night from motor-powered boats. The catch is landed at dawn and sold in the markets of the towns of Qizan and Sabya. Spanish mackerel is the main source of protein in the diet here.

The influence of nearby Africa is seen in the conical houses built in clusters. High reed fences surround the groups of buildings. The single-room units are lined with mud and painted inside with designs.

Market day, sometimes only once a week, is an important time for people to get together, trade, and share news. Food and manufactured goods are sold, but so are local products such as straw hats and baskets, keys or nails made of iron from nearby mines, and salt that comes from the Eastern Province.

Hospitality, important in all regions, is shown when entertaining guests. The usual lamb and rice is likely to be served.

29

A baker with freshly baked bread

A special dish from this region is *arikah,* bread that is broken off and fashioned into the shape of a spoon to be dipped into a side dish of honey.

EASTERN

From the low coastal strip along the Persian Gulf, with its sand and salt flats, the Eastern Province includes sand plains and dunes, rock plateaus, and large sections of the Rub' al-Khali, the largest continuous sand area in the world. For many years this territory was cut off from contact with the rest of Saudi Arabia. Caravans were few and the area had a tough reputation.

Many of the people who came to this land came by way of the Persian Gulf. This population from the outside did not have tribal links and were subject to the tribal groups of the interior.

The tribes that lived inland faced an especially harsh territory. The heat and shortage of food for animals forced some Bedouin to move their camps every few days. Their food was the milk of their animals, some meat, dates, and small amounts of rice or unleavened bread. Yet these people enjoyed their independence

The port of Dammam (left) and the University of Petroleum and Minerals (right)

and their freedom of movement so much that today they have found it difficult to adjust to modern development.

The farmers in the province have had better food and shelter. The area around Hufuf has a good water supply, beautiful gardens, and large palm groves. Fortunately good underground water supplies have helped support the rapidly growing cities of the area.

Oil was first discovered in the Eastern Province and brought new prosperity to the region. The port of Dammam was once a fishing village with a side industry of pearl diving. Now it is an important business center. Nearby is Dhahran, a center for the oil industry. The University of Petroleum and Minerals trains new managers and technicians for this industry.

Although bound together by many ancient traditions, the people of Saudi Arabia have been shaped by the different conditions in the territories in which they live. They are a people who have experienced great change in the twentieth century as they acquired oil wealth. Yet they also place great weight in their heritage and their history.

Chapter 3

BIRTHPLACE OF MUHAMMAD, PROPHET OF ISLAM

Perhaps the most spectacular time in the history of the territory that was to become Saudi Arabia was the seventh century A.D. This was the time of Muhammad, Prophet of Islam, and the expansion of Islam to a world power. However, the pre-Islamic history also is important. With the establishment of a government department of antiquities and expeditions of archaeological teams in the country, new discoveries may be made that will enhance our knowledge of the role this territory played in early civilizations.

PREHISTORY

Trying to find out what a country was like before written records requires patient detective work—making deductions from the few clues that are found. From objects that have been discovered, archaeologists have deduced certain facts. Three areas of human settlement were along the coastlines to the east, west, and south. The oldest, dating to about 5000 B.C., was found some fifty-six miles (ninety kilometers) north of Dhahran on the Persian Gulf. These artifacts are like those discovered in

A street in Hufuf

Mesopotamia (now Iraq), where an ancient civilization was established along the banks of the Tigris and Euphrates rivers. The people who produced these artifacts were the ancestors of the Sumerians, the first people known to have established cities.

Did these ancient Mesopotamians come to the Arabian Peninsula to establish a colony? Or did humans come from Arabia to settle in the more fertile river valleys? We do not have the answer to these questions, but the Sumerians had a myth that agriculture had been brought to them by a "fish man" from the Persian Gulf. If the myth carries a hint of the truth, then perhaps people migrating from Arabia carried with them the knowledge of farming.

From 4000 to 2000 B.C., there was a civilization centered around a city called Dilmun that controlled some 250 miles (402 kilometers) of territory along the eastern coast of present-day Kuwait and the island of Bahrain and extended inland some 56 miles (90 kilometers) to what is now the oasis of Hufuf. Dilmun controlled trade routes between Mesopotamia and the Indus Valley in present-day India. Dilmun was considered a holy city by the Mesopotamians.

What was happening in the central part of the peninsula? Some scholars speculate that until about 3000 B.C. the climate had sufficient rain to support people who grew cereal crops and herded animals in the north and people who hunted and gathered food in the south. However, as the climate became drier, these people could no longer maintain their way of life and were forced to move to the oases, to the coasts, or away from Arabia.

Migrations of people played an important role in ancient civilizations. It seems that about every thousand years people were forced out of the Arabian Peninsula because the population grew too large or the people needed to follow the wild animals who were a food source. The people then settled in areas along the major rivers. In about 3500 B.C., people who spoke a Semitic language spilled out of Arabia by two routes. One road took them north to the Sinai Peninsula and into Egypt and the settlements along the Nile River. The other route was east to Sumer (in present-day Iraq) in Mesopotamia along the Tigris and Euphrates rivers. These people may well have enriched the Egyptian and Babylonian civilizations. Another wave of migration around 2500 B.C. may have added to the Canaanite and Phoenician cultures, civilizations from the eastern Mediterranean coast. Around 1500 to 1200 B.C. more migrants, who became the ancestors of the Aramaeans, the Syrians, and the Jews, may have poured into Syria and Palestine.

CARAVAN TRADE

Two very important products were to attract people back to the Arabian Peninsula. Southern Arabia produced two gum resins: frankincense and myrrh. Frankincense was incense that was burned in religious rituals. It also was used in cremation services and for embalming. Myrrh was used as a foundation for cosmetics

An ancient illustration of an Arab caravan

and perfumes and as a medicine. It was very expensive, but demand for the product was great.

At first, trade in these products was controlled by Egyptians or the civilizations in Mesopotamia. However, the value of these products attracted a reverse migration of people from what is now eastern Jordan and southern Iraq back to Arabia. These settlers came around 1500 B.C. and again in 1200 B.C., bringing with them the culture of their former homelands. They knew how to organize cities and how to irrigate. They had advanced techniques in working with metal and ceramics. They used an alphabetic script. Their religion and art was brought from their home countries. These people developed their own kingdoms.

During the first century B.C., these kingdoms were formed into a loose confederation. While there may have been some fighting among themselves, their geographic isolation made them relatively safe from outside attack. They did not build fortifications around their towns. They worshiped three gods and were ruled by a priest king. Later this ruler became more secular and governed through chiefs who controlled settled tribes. Unlike the northern tribes that were grouped according to family relationships, these tribes were organized by commercial or labor interests.

Indian and Arab merchants trading at an Arab port

These kingdoms were populated by great traders and middlemen. In addition to their own products, they sold goods from India and Africa. Their customers assumed that Arabia was the source of the pearls, spices (used to preserve and flavor food), swords, silks, slaves, monkeys, ivory, gold, and ostrich feathers. Thus they gave the area the name of *Arabia Felix*, or "Happy Arabia."

The southern part of the peninsula was the only section that was able to grow all its own food, thanks to an irrigation system that utilized the runoff water from rain. Dams were used to direct the water into irrigation systems.

Because the Red Sea had dangerous wind conditions, navigation was difficult. Goods coming by sea were transferred to camel caravans to be carried partway by land. Caravan cities to the north were established as colonies. Later these towns, such as Mecca and Medina, assumed control of trading ventures. Increased trade became possible because camels were now present in the area and were used for transportation. (Originally, camels were domesticated as dairy animals in southern Arabia.)

Trade was too lucrative to go unchallenged. The caravan cities began to assume more power. Then the Greeks and the Romans came on the scene as competitors. Greek sailors from Alexandria in Egypt learned how to sail the Red Sea and travel on to India. The secret was out that the fabulous trade items were not the products of Arabia. The spread of Christianity, with its prohibition of cremation, decreased the demand for frankincense. Southern Arabia went into a serious slump.

After the fall of Jerusalem in A.D. 70, many Jews fled to the Arabian Peninsula and made converts to Judaism in their new homeland. Later, Christian missionaries moved into the territory and also began making converts. By the fourth century Christianity was established. In 523 a leader who had converted to Judaism had Christians massacred at Najran. The Christians appealed for help from the Byzantine Empire. The Byzantines referred the request to the Abyssinians, the nearest Christian ally. An Abyssinian protectorate was established in 570, only to be replaced five years later by a Persian government that the Jews and Arabians considered preferable.

MUHAMMAD AND THE SPREAD OF ISLAM

Muhammad, the Prophet of Islam, was born in 570 in Mecca. The Quraysh tribe to which he belonged was the leading tribe of this caravan city. It had power through its control of the spice trade, its knowledge of tribal politics, and its skill at camel warfare. The tribe received payment from the merchants in return for some protection of the caravans. The business required a careful assessment of the profit margin of the merchants and the money needed to buy off the tribes along the route.

The Quraysh had originated in the north. There a camel saddle had been invented, permitting the rider to sit above the hump of the animal. This position afforded better control of the animal and better use of the spear and the sword. While the camel was required for desert travel, the horse was a superior animal in a fight because it could be maneuvered more easily. Tribes would raid each other to secure horses. There was almost constant fighting between tribes before the time of Muhammad.

An annual truce of four months had been agreed on among the northern tribes to allow the people to engage in religious observances and trading. These people believed in spirits and demons, especially those associated with nature. They worshiped some gods and goddesses and had the idea of a supreme God.

There were many altars and shrines. In Mecca the Ka'ba, a temple housing a meteorite, was considered especially sacred. Just southeast of Mecca was the site of the Ukaz fair where the annual poetry contest was held and where the tribes met to trade and catch up on news. The poetry often exalted a hero. There were prophets who promised the coming of a great leader.

Shortly before Muhammad's birth, his father died. According to custom, the child Muhammad was sent to a Bedouin family. Life in the desert was thought to produce strength of character and good health. When Muhammad was five years old, he was brought home to live with his mother, who had a small estate. However, his mother died shortly thereafter, and Muhammad was looked after by his grandfather. When his grandfather died two years later, his uncle took over responsibility for him.

When Muhammad was twenty-five years old his uncle

The Arabic script on the Saudi state flag reads: "There is no God but God; Muhammad is the messenger of God."

introduced him to a forty-two-year-old widow of their tribe. Khadija was a prosperous businesswoman who equipped caravans for their journey to Syria. She hired Muhammad to lead one of the caravans. Shortly afterward, they were married. Muhammad went from a fairly humble position in the tribe to one of wealth. Khadija and Muhammad had six children. Their four daughters were healthy, but their two sons died as infants. Although custom would have permitted Muhammad to take another wife, he did not do so until after Khadija's death.

Muhammad was troubled about much that he saw in Mecca. Tribal traditions of hospitality and generosity were giving way to greed. The pilgrims who came to worship at the Ka'ba, with its 360 idols, were confronted by traders selling souvenirs and magical protections. Muhammad often went to a cave in the nearby desert to meditate.

When he was about forty, around the year 610, Muhammad

Muslims take off their shoes before they bow in prayer.

reported that he had been visited by the angel Gabriel who gave him a revelation about the nature of God. Muhammad went home and told Khadija what had happened and questioned whether or not he was going mad. His wife consulted her cousin, and they encouraged Muhammad to wait for further revelations. Over many months, Muhammad received more revelations. He was told that he was a messenger to instruct others. These revelations were collected in the *Qur'an*, the holy book of the Muslims, sometimes spelled Koran.

At first, except for his wife and a few friends, Muhammad was dismissed as harmless and not to be taken seriously. However, as he preached about the evil that would come to those who did not follow his teaching, he became more of a problem for his tribe. The leaders of his tribe felt that Muhammad's proclamation of monotheism (belief in one God) could disrupt the profitable pilgrimages to the idols of Mecca. Muhammad's emphasis on the brotherhood of faith could undercut the blood ties of the tribe. His concern for the poor could lead the poor to expect too much from the rich.

The leaders of the Quraysh tribe tried to get Muhammad's uncle to eject him from the family clan, the Hashim, a subgroup of the Quraysh. Although the uncle was not a convert, he refused. The Hashim clan was boycotted by the other members of the tribe. Muhammad went to nearby Ta'if to try to win support, but the groups there physically ousted him.

The only tribe that seemed interested was from Yathrib (later to be called Medina). Leaders of that tribe thought that Muhammad might be able to settle some of the blood feuds that existed in their town. They offered Muhammad and his converts a place to live. Muhammad and some two hundred people left in small groups and migrated to Medina. This trip is called the *hijra*. It took courage for these converts to leave Mecca and the protection of their families. July 16, 622, has been designated as the day that Muhammad left Mecca—a date that was later specified as the start of the Muslim calendar.

Medina, meaning "the city," provided Muhammad with security, position, and a place to consolidate his political plans. Raiding caravans from Mecca was a tactic that helped to provide economic support for the followers of Muhammad. It also weakened the enemies who had opposed him.

The fighting between the people of Mecca and the followers of Muhammad, called Muslims, escalated. There were victories on both sides. However, the Muslims were highly disciplined fighters who did not fear death. When they were fighting in a holy war, known as *jihad,* they had the promise of a place in paradise if they died. If they lived and won, they gained the plunder of war.

The people of Mecca tired of having their wealthy caravan trade disrupted, so in 627 they marched out with ten thousand men to lay siege to Medina. When they reached their target, they found that a huge ditch had been dug wherever the city might be attacked with horses. Although the Meccans tried several assaults, they were unsuccessful. Because they were running low on food and water they retreated and lost the Battle of the Ditch. The Meccans lost more than just this battle. The tribes, seeing the defeat of Mecca, began giving their allegiance to Muhammad.

During the Battle of the Ditch, a Jewish tribe from Medina collaborated with the Meccans. In earlier fights some of the Jewish residents had been expelled because of disloyalty. Now, the remaining Jews were killed or sold into slavery.

From his new position of strength, Muhammad negotiated a truce so that he could visit Mecca on a pilgrimage. He gained new converts while there. In 630, he returned to Mecca with an armed force of ten thousand. The people of Mecca surrendered and decided to submit and embrace Islam. No reprisals were taken. The idols were removed from the Ka'ba.

Pilgrimage to Mecca at least once in a lifetime was and is expected of all Muslims who can travel there. This pilgrimage is called the *hajj*. Caravan trading resumed under the protection of the Muslims. The one new financial obligation was the *zakat* (almsgiving), the contribution to the poor.

Muhammad returned to Medina. More of the Arabian tribes flocked to his banner. For the first time, most of the peninsula was united under a single leader. Only a short time later, in 632, Muhammad, now more than sixty years old, became ill and died.

According to the tradition accepted by most Muslims, no provision had been made for Muhammad's successor. Under the tribal system, leadership was decided by consensus. The Medinans put forward one candidate; the early converts from Mecca backed another. The successful compromise candidate was Abu Bakr, the

earliest supporter of Muhammad outside his family. However, the
faction that backed Ali, the other candidate, claimed the
leadership vote should have fallen to Ali because he was
Muhammad's cousin and nearest male relative. Ali had married
Fatima, the daughter of Muhammad, and had fathered the
Prophet's two grandsons. The question of this leadership still
divides Muslims today. The Shi'ites claim Ali as the rightful
leader, while the Sunnis accept Abu Bakr.

Abu Bakr, as the first *caliph*, "successor," the political as well as
the spiritual leader, had to deal with the defection of many of the
tribes who claimed that their pledge of loyalty was to Muhammad
and not to Islam, the Muslim faith. Muslim generals brought the
stragglers back into the fold, and the rule of Islam in Arabia was
secured. Moreover, the faith had pushed into the neighboring
lands of Syria and Iraq. All this was accomplished within two
years of Muhammad's death.

Led by generals like the famous tactician Khalid ibn al-Walid,
the Arabs began the spread of their power. They challenged the
Byzantine Empire in the west and the Sassanian Persian Empire in
the east. Eventually they were to sweep across Africa and into
Spain to the Atlantic Ocean and across India and on to the Pacific
Ocean. The center of power of the great Islamic Empire was
moved first to the ancient city of Damascus (Syria) and then to the
newly established city of Baghdad (Iraq). Arabia was left behind—
still the home of the Holy Cities of Mecca and Medina to which
pilgrimage must be made, but away from the center of decision
making.

As other areas were conquered, the religion of Islam was
introduced. Trade also brought the Islamic religion to new
territories and missionaries tried to convert others.

The Saud family lived in
Diriyeh in the central
part of Arabia. It was
here that Muhammad ibn
Abd al-Wahhab was welcomed
and protected by
Ibn Saud. The entrance
to the Saud ancestral home
is on the left.

Chapter 4

THE SAUD FAMILY AND
THE WAHHABIS

History is often told from the vantage point of the winners. Today, the Saud family rules Saudi Arabia and the Wahhabis are the important religious force. Therefore the origins of these two families are significant, even though they were perhaps not a major factor at the time.

EARLY HISTORY OF THE SAUDS AND THE WAHHABIS

Around 1450 the Saud family moved inland from the Qatif oasis near the Persian Gulf to Najd in the central part of Arabia. They established date-palm plantations and supplied pilgrimage caravans with camels, food, and water. Although the family prospered, life was not all that secure. Tribal raids could wipe out accumulated wealth. The sharifs (direct descendants of the Prophet Muhammad through his daughter Fatima) who ruled in Mecca and Medina were an important power in the area. The sharifs ruled under the control first of the Mamluks of Egypt and Syria, and later under the Ottoman Turks. As long as the sharifs sent a share of their trade profits to the rulers of these empires and remained loyal to them, the sharifs could do pretty much what they pleased. They ruled until 1925.

Meanwhile various European countries with sailing and

business skills took an interest in the lucrative trade through the Red Sea. First it was the Portuguese in the fifteenth century. Then the Mamluks moved their armies into southwest Arabia and exacted a heavy price from the people, especially around Jiddah. By 1517, the Ottomans had conquered the Mamluks and established their rule in Egypt and Syria. The Bani Khalid tribe liberated the eastern coast of the peninsula from the Ottomans around 1669. The trading routes in the Red Sea and the Persian Gulf were controlled first by the Dutch and then the British. The sharifs of the Hijaz managed to get along with these groups and retain their wealth and local control.

Islam was still strong in the Hijaz around the Holy Cities. However, in the rest of Arabia, a worship of natural objects had become mixed with Islamic practices. With tribes on the move, teaching religion was not always easy, and the transmission of the faith was contaminated by old beliefs. A religious leader—Muhammad ibn Abd al-Wahhab—arose to challenge this condition and urge a return to the teachings of Muhammad and Islamic law and the abandonment of pagan superstitions.

Abd al-Wahhab's early interest in religious matters was encouraged by his family. They sent him to study Islamic law in a number of cities famed for their theological schools. However, because of his criticism of local religious practices, he was considered a fanatic and expelled from Basra (in present-day Iraq). Abd al-Wahhab felt Muslims had become lax. He was against any practices that were not approved by the Qur'an or the Prophet Muhammad. When he returned to his home, his preaching met with opposition from the local leaders and he was expelled from his village in 1744 by the Bani Khalid tribe.

Muhammad ibn Saud, who later became king of Saudi Arabia, gave Abd al-Wahhab physical protection and became his ally. The two planned a jihad to purify and conquer the rest of Arabia. In 1765, at the time of Muhammad ibn Saud's death, most of the Najd were Wahhabis. The Wahhabis follow a strict interpretation of the Qur'an.

The alliance of the two families had been cemented by a number of intermarriages, including that of the daughter of Abd al-Wahhab to Muhammad ibn Saud. The religious leader continued his alliance with the next leader of the Saud family, Abd al-Aziz. They conquered Riyadh, the city that was to become the capital of Saudi Arabia.

The success of the Wahhabi movement was a threat to the other powers in the area. Expansion out of the Najd was blocked on the east by the powerful raiding Bani Khalid tribe. The sharifs on the southwest banned the Wahhabis from coming to the Holy Cities. Still farther southwest, the Isma'ilis, who were a Shi'ite Muslim group, began to attack the Najd. To the north, the Muntafiqis, an Iraqi tribal group, invaded. However, some of the Muntafiqis converted to Wahhabism and joined forces with the Wahhabis.

The control of the Wahhabis was gradually extended—both by peaceful persuasion and by the sword. By 1792 and the death of Abd al-Wahhab, control had been established south to the Rub' al-Khali. Through conquest of the oases of Qatif and Hufuf, the Hasa area was forced to accept Wahhabism. In 1801, Karbala, the Shi'ite holy city in what is now Iraq, was attacked. The tomb of a religious leader was stripped of its jewels and the territory was looted. By the time of the death of Abd al-Aziz in 1803, the route between Najd and the Hijaz was more under the control of the

Wahhabis than the forces of the sharifs. Moreover, a key oasis was controlled by the Wahhabis.

These victories were not enough without the control of the Hijaz. The Wahhabis pushed on and took Mecca in 1801 and Medina in 1805. The reformers attacked the tombs of the saints and anything else that was perceived to conflict with the worship of the one God. The Sharif Ghalib was allowed to continue administering the area. Saud, the new leader, now had the task of governing the larger territory under his control. Islamic law and judges were installed in villages and cities. Tribal feuds were to be settled by a central Wahhabi power. District governors were placed in forts surrounded by moats located outside the conquered towns.

THE RESPONSE OF THE OTTOMAN EMPIRE

While squabbles in Arabia might not have been worth the Ottomans' attention, the conquest of Mecca and Medina was another matter. The Ottomans, who were Muslims, stood to lose both prestige and money if they did not challenge this new development. Muhammad Ali, the viceroy for the empire in Cairo, Egypt, then part of the Ottoman Empire, was given the task of retaking the cities. While the Saudi family was fighting over leadership on the death of Saud, Abd Allah, Saud's son, was captured and killed by the Ottomans. The family regrouped around Abd Allah's uncle, Turki ibn Abd Allah. From his base in Riyadh, Turki ibn Abd Allah organized troops and drove the Egyptians from the Najd. However, to be left in peace by the Egyptians, Turki agreed to pay an annual tribute to Egypt. Turki

Muhammad Ali

recognized the importance of Wahhabism as a nationalistic movement to counter foreign occupation. When Turki was assassinated in 1834 by a rival from the family, his son Faisal took control.

Both Faisal and his cousin, Khalid ibn Saud, had been Egyptian prisoners, but Faisal had escaped in 1828. The internal weakness of the family created opportunities for their enemies. Qatar, Bahrain, and the Bani Khalid tribe of Hasa revolted.

Muhammad Ali, who no longer worked for the Ottomans, decided to bring Arabia into his orbit. He used Khalid ibn Saud, making him ruler in the Najd, and for the second time Faisal became an Egyptian prisoner.

The British refused to let Muhammad Ali into Yemen on the south and he had difficulty trying to consolidate his gains in central Arabia. This persuaded Muhammad Ali to withdraw in

1840. When Faisal again escaped from Egypt in 1843, he resumed his position as leader. Faisal tried to restore order and take care of problems among the Bedouin. He was concerned about the safety of pilgrimages and encouraged business and agriculture.

The prosperity that lasted for some twenty-two years was destroyed by the civil wars that arose following Faisal's death in 1865. Three of his sons, Abd Allah, Saud, and Abd al-Rahman, fought for power while their land suffered anarchy, famine, tribal war, and invasion by the Ottomans. The family of Muhammad ibn Rashid, an administrator whom the Saudis had put in charge in the north, gained power over much of the Najd and in 1891 forced Abd al-Rahman out of Riyadh. The exiled ruler fled to Kuwait with his family, including his eleven-year-old son, Abd al-Aziz (later to be known as Ibn Saud), who eventually was to regain power and found the modern nation of Saudi Arabia.

Meanwhile European colonial powers such as Britain and France were concerned about protecting and extending their business interests in the area. Great Britain was especially active in the coastal areas of Arabia in establishing treaties and alliances to protect British trade with India.

IBN SAUD

In 1902 the son of Abd al-Rahman, Ibn Saud, led fifty men in a raid on Riyadh at dawn. The father bestowed his title of *amir*, "prince," on his son while keeping the religious title of *imam*. The title of imam was not used after Abd al-Rahman's death. Thus power was consolidated in one person, the amir. Ibn Saud, now the leader of his tribe, went on to defeat the Rashidis and their

Ibn Saud (left) and King Hussein (right)

Turkish allies from Hasa. Ibn Saud had to acknowledge the
Ottoman claim to the area because Hussein, a Hashemite Sharif of
Mecca backed by the Ottomans, was holding one of his brothers
hostage. When the boy was released, the Saudis forgot about
Ottoman claims and seized the territory from Kuwait to Qatar, as
well as the Najd.

A revival of Wahhabism helped to cement the loyalty of the
Bedouin to the Saud family. Tribesmen were encouraged to settle
in the agricultural oases so that they could be taught the Wahhabi
ideas and be available as warriors. The term *Ikhwan*, "brothers" or
"brethren," was applied to the settlers and the organization that
was formed. By 1916 all Bedouin tribes were ordered to join the
Ikhwan and pay the zakat tax for the poor. The tribal leaders were

required to attend the schools in law and religion at Riyadh. The leaders were then invited to stay at this city and become members of Ibn Saud's court. In this way, the tribesmen might be expected to be loyal to the Saudis and the Ikhwan movement.

During World War I there was conflict in the Middle East and in Arabia. The Rashidis became the allies of the Ottoman Turks, whereas the Hashemites sought recognition of their independence through cooperation with the British. The British tried to get Ibn Saud to fight against the Ottomans. Ibn Saud refused, indicating that his forces were not yet ready for such a battle. He did not want to take a back seat to the Hashemite Hussein. The British settled for recognizing Ibn Saud as amir of Najd and Hasa and provided a subsidy to encourage him to fight against the Rashidis and to prevent attacks on Hussein. Hussein, with assistance from British officers like T. E. Lawrence (known as Lawrence of Arabia), pushed the Turks out of the Hijaz and back to Damascus. Ibn Saud did not attack the Hijaz but consolidated his control over areas vacated by the allies of the Turks, all the way to the border of the Rashidi capital of Ha'il in the north central section of Saudi Arabia.

After World War I, the British and French rewarded Hussein by seeing that one of his sons, Faisal, was made king of Iraq and another son, Abd Allah, king of Transjordan. When the two Hashemite sons started negotiating with the Rashidis, Ibn Saud seized Ha'il with his Ikhwan forces in 1921. He married the widow of Saud ibn Rashid and adopted her children, thereby winning allegiance from the Rashidis.

Then the Ikhwan, successful in raiding along the border of Transjordan, crossed over the border and massacred the inhabitants of a Transjordanian town. The British responded with

Prince Faisal (in foreground) and T. E. Lawrence (second from right in middle row) were delegates to the Peace Conference of 1919 in Paris.

air power, driving off most of the Ikhwan. Ibn Saud was angry and ordered the Ikhwan survivors killed as punishment for their attack on the town.

Ibn Saud was involved in negotiations with a British diplomat over the borders with Iraq and Kuwait. Borders and agreed neutral zones were fixed at this time.

Now Ibn Saud made his move against the Hijaz, which his Ikhwan wanted because of the Holy Cities. One of his sons, Faisal, attacked and conquered the territory of Asir. Hussein had become unpopular in his own territory because of his high taxes, for which the residents received little in return. When Hussein declared himself caliph of all Muslims and was not supported by the Islamic world, Ibn Saud and his Ikhwan warriors moved into the Hijaz and conquered the cities of Mecca and Medina.

The British wanted to support Ibn Saud but had to settle the boundary disagreements between the Saudis and the other British allies in the region. The Treaty of Jiddah in 1927 established Saudi authority from the Persian Gulf to the Red Sea, but also limited expansion into areas held by others. In the same year, Ibn Saud was enthroned as king of the Hijaz and Najd.

Some of the Ikhwan did not want to give up their raiding into Iraq and felt that the introduction of modern inventions such as cars and telephones was against their religion. At the Battle of Sibila in 1929, the king put down the revolt and transferred many of his fighters to the newly established regular army. In 1932 Ibn Saud renamed his land the Kingdom of Saudi Arabia.

While Ibn Saud remained committed to the Wahhabi idea of Islam, he knew that if his nation was to survive it would have to take advantage of modern technology. He had to balance the demands of modernization and religious practice. Committees were formed to encourage good religious observances and to eliminate practices such as smoking, singing, and drinking alcohol. In 1926 there was legislation that secular law could supplement the *Sharia*, the religious law. In 1929, the king hosted a pan-Islamic conference in Mecca to regulate pilgrimages and to show other Muslims that he could be a responsible administrator of the Holy Cities.

While the king ruled as an absolute monarch, he remained accessible to his people and listened to other tribal leaders. He made every effort to do away with tribal rivalries and entered into more then twenty marriage alliances with women from other tribes in furtherance of this policy.

Money was a problem. The British subsidies ended after World War I. During World War II the Italians bombed oil fields and the trade that catered to pilgrims was nearly eliminated. Not until after 1944 did the oil revenues exceed four million dollars. Then oil developers began pouring money into the kingdom. At first there was too little to go around in a country that had so many needs. By the time of Ibn Saud's death in 1953, when revenue from oil money had grown to an amazing amount, the waste of

King Ibn Saud (right) and King Abdullah of Transjordan (left) met in 1948 to discuss Palestine.

money by some of the royal family and the slow development of social services in the country brought criticism from outsiders and discontent within. Probably the harshest critics were other Arabs.

An original member of the Arab League, formed in 1945, Saudi Arabia sent a small force to support the fighting against Israel in 1948 when the British withdrew from Palestine and Israel declared its independence and claimed territory there. In disputes among the Arabs, Saudi Arabia tended to side with Egypt and Syria against the old family enemies in Jordan and Iraq.

Ibn Saud had been a remarkable leader, from the time he, as a twenty-one-year-old, led the raid reversing his family's fortune to the end of his reign in Saudi Arabia in the twentieth century. He had tried to bring tribal conflicts under control and bring modernization that would not undermine the values of Islam. However, the style of leadership that had created the Kingdom of Saudi Arabia had to be modified to deal with the new conditions in the nation and the world.

CHANGE AFTER THE DEATH OF IBN SAUD

When the king died on November 9, 1953, Saudi Arabia had to get used to new rulers and adapt to changes taking place in the world. From among the king's many sons, Saud ibn Abd al-Aziz,

Ibn Saud (seated) was succeeded by his son Saud ibn Abd al-Aziz (standing)

who had been the crown prince, was selected by the royal family to be the next king. Another son, Faisal ibn Abd al-Aziz, was chosen to become the crown prince and prime minister. The two sons were quite different in temperament. The new king inherited his father's sense of gaiety and humor, while his brother, the crown prince, was more like his father in piety, austerity, and a realistic understanding of human beings. There was tension between the two brothers and the crown prince resigned. However, the royal family, concerned that Saud was letting the now prosperous kingdom go to ruin, stepped in. With the backing of religious leaders, they removed the apparently ill and extravagant Saud and installed his brother Faisal as ruler.

Faisal ruled from 1964 until March 25, 1975 when he was assassinated by one of his nephews. Fears that the nephew might

King Faisal (left) and King Fahd (right)

have acted as part of a conspiracy proved unfounded upon
investigation. The prince who was guilty of the murder was
executed.

King Faisal was followed by his half-brother, Khalid ibn Abd
al-Aziz, who became king and prime minister. The new crown
prince and first deputy prime minister was another of the
brothers, Fahd ibn Abd al-Aziz. When King Khalid died on June
13, 1982 after a long illness, his younger brother, the present King
Fahd, who had been crown prince, took over as king. All these
questions of succession were determined by the leaders within the
royal family, much as the decision would be made about the
leadership within a Bedouin tribe.

Throughout this period a number of issues required the
attention of these rulers. New ministries and a cabinet were
formed to facilitate the rule of the vast territory that had been
consolidated by Ibn Saud. National and foreign interests in the
petroleum industry had to be considered. The wish for new
technologies such as movies and television had to be evaluated in
light of religious teachings. The national budget could vary

depending on the price and demand for oil. The money had to accommodate the needs of the expanding royal family as the next generations produced children. Funds also had to support the social service needs of the country as a whole.

The role of Saudi Arabia among the Arab nations and the countries of the world was a primary concern of the rulers. Saudi Arabia did not join either the United Arab Republic (the alliance of Egypt and Syria) or the opposing Arab Federation (alliance of Iraq and Jordan). The revolution in neighboring Yemen and the sweep of part of that country into the Soviet orbit was considered a serious threat. The various wars between Arab nations and Israel and the growing military strength of Israel resulted in Saudi support of the Arab nations on the frontline of hostilities. Saudi Arabia also supplied financial backing to Iraq in its war against Iran. Saudi Arabia in conjunction with other Arab nations has tried to find an Arab solution to the conflict in Lebanon.

The presence of Mecca in Saudi Arabia with the pilgrimage of other Muslims into the area has created difficulties on several occasions. In 1979, 250 armed followers of a Sunni extremist leader occupied the Grand Mosque; they were defeated by Saudi troops and 229 people were killed. Then in 1987, there were armed clashes between Iranian pilgrims who followed the Shi'ite Ayatollah Khomeini and the Saudi forces, with 402 killed. To deal with future arrangements for the pilgrims, the Saudis announced that they would establish a quota of 1,000 persons for every million citizens from each Muslim national community.

Fine-tuning oil production and prices with other producing countries of the Organization of Petroleum Exporting Countries (OPEC) is of great importance to the Saudis. While oil supplies have been used as a weapon by Arab members of OPEC unhappy

OPEC oil ministers meeting at their Vienna, Austria, headquarters in 1988

with Western support for Israel, curtailment of oil can work against the interests of the OPEC countries if it forces the shift to other fuel sources or if it upsets the world economy. Often Saudi Arabia has urged moderation with regard to cutting off supplies to Western countries to avoid harm to the national interests of the oil-exporting countries.

Saudi relations with the United States have been close because of the substantial involvement of American companies in development and production of the Saudi oil fields. The United States was considered a better risk by the Saudis than the British whose imperial designs were feared and who were geographically closer. Also, many of the Saudi royal family have attended universities in the United States. The United States has been consulted for advice and for arms for military defenses. However, when the United States Congress refused to approve an arms deal with the Saudis, they turned to Great Britain for an even larger deal.

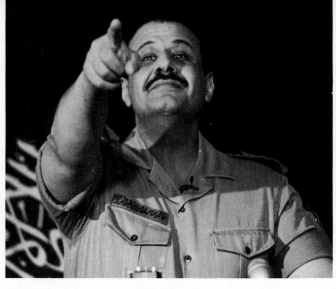

Above: Saudi Prince Lieutenant-General Khalid ibn Sultan served as commander during the Persian Gulf War. Left: A Saudi soldier faces Mecca and prays.

When Saddam Hussein, president of Iraq, marched his army into Kuwait and threatened Saudi Arabia in 1990, the United Nations and the Arab League voted their condemnation of the aggression. At the invitation of the Saudi rulers, a coalition of Western and Arab troops from twenty-seven nations were moved into the eastern part of Saudi Arabia to protect the Saudi borders.

When the Persian Gulf War began in January 1991, it was from Saudi airfields that many of the planes thundered off to bomb Baghdad, Iraq's capital. Arab forces were under the command of Saudi Prince Lieutenant-General Khalid ibn Sultan.

On January 29, 1991 seven hundred Iraqi troops with tanks and artillery rockets invaded Saudi Arabia. They took the town of Khafji that was just south of the border and had been almost abandoned by civilians because of the danger. Saudi troops, with those of Qatar, pushed back the invaders by January 31. The Iraqis had tried to claim a great victory. However, the Khafji conflict gave coalition forces an opportunity to size up the maneuvers and the quality of Iraq's equipment.

Left: Oil wells in Kuwait
burned out of control.
Above: A Saudi examines an area
polluted from oil spills.

When the coalition began the ground war, the Saudi forces moved into Kuwait. At the successful conclusion of the one-hundred-hour war, Kuwait was liberated with a very small loss of life to the coalition forces.

The "environmental terrorism" of Saddam Hussein in releasing oil from tankers and pipelines into the Persian Gulf and in setting fire to the oil wells in Kuwait will have long-range consequences. The gulf is shallow (average depth is 110 feet; 33.5 meters) and the water is exchanged only slowly with the Indian Ocean. The oil spill was timed to coincide with shrimp spawning and seabird migration. Efforts were made to keep the oil away from the desalination water plants as well as water-cooled refinery and electrical plants.

The oil fires raised threats to health because the smoke can trigger bronchitis and asthma problems and may lead to an increase in cancer. Acid rain and even a possible change in climate are also dangers.

King Fahd in August 1991

Saudi Arabia emerged from the Gulf War a stronger power. There was slight physical damage except around Khafji and a few buildings hit by Iraqi scud missiles. However, the forty-eight billion dollars that the nation contributed represented nearly half of its annual gross domestic product. The nation took out a loan for the first time in twenty years.

What will happen to the domestic situation in Saudi Arabia is not clear. Some Saudis want more liberalization and modernization of their country. Conservatives, alarmed at the presence of so many foreigners and their influence in their country, are asking for an even stricter application of Islamic law. King Fahd and the royal family, who have become even stronger with the successful conclusion of the war, hold a center position.

Saudi Arabia has survived since the death of Ibn Saud in 1953. This nation with its oil wealth and its role within the Arab community is of prime importance to all industrialized countries.

Chapter 5

THE KINGDOM OF SAUDI ARABIA

The importance of religion in Saudi Arabia is symbolized by the flag of the nation. The flag contains a sword and the Arabic script of the credo of Islam: "There is no god but God, and Muhammad is the messenger of God."

GOVERNMENT

Saudi Arabia is usually given the classification of absolute monarchy because it has no legislature or political parties. However, the Saudis are quick to point out that their king is not like the absolute monarchs of Asiatic countries. The king as a Muslim is an ordinary person. Only God is considered great. Saudis do not bow to their king. He rules subject to Islamic law, the Sharia, and therefore does not have unlimited power.

Saudi Arabia has no written constitution. Except for foreign workers, the population is Muslim. Some claim that the country is more like a theocracy because of the imposition of Islam on all the inhabitants. While foreigners may pursue their own life-style in private, when they are out in Saudi society they are expected to conform.

In 1992 the king issued a series of royal decrees that decentralized power and established a bill of rights for the first time. It should be noted that these decrees can be changed only through another royal decree. The eighty-three articles of these royal decrees are called the "Basic System of Government."

Opposition to a constitution and a legislature has been based on religious principles. The new decrees state that all changes to be made are based on the Qur'an and the Sharia. Saudis believe that only God can issue law, so they have adopted orders or regulations formed into codes to deal with certain economic or social questions. The oil arrangements with the West have been handled mostly by contracts. To meet certain expectations of other nations, slavery was declared abolished in 1962. These arrangements were approved by the religious leaders on the grounds that they were not prohibited by the Sharia.

In the past Muslims who did not conform to acceptable behavior in public were pestered by enforcers of the Wahhabi way of life — called the religious police. Foreign magazines were censored, and advertisements for alcohol and pictures of women considered not properly clad were blacked out. Whether the new decrees to protect individual liberties will stem these practices remains to be seen.

The Qur'an orders leaders to take counsel among themselves. Consultation and the building of consensus have been especially important for the royal family to remain in power and present a united front. In 1992 this principle of consultation has been formalized with the creation of a Consultative Council.

The council consists of sixty members and a president, chosen by the king. The rights and duties of the members are set by royal decree. Members must be of Saudi nationality, birth, and origin, be known as persons of virtue and ability, and be at least thirty years of age.

The council has a four-year term, and a new council is to be formed two months before the end of the existing council. Persons who have not served in the previous council will make up at least half of the new council. However, the king may disband the council and appoint a new one at any time.

The purpose of the council is to give its opinion on matters referred to it by the prime minister. The council reviews development plans, gives opinions about agreements and alliances, and debates annual reports submitted by government organizations.

Resolutions are valid if adopted by a majority with a two-thirds quorum of the membership present. The council can form committees, hire experts, require testimony of government officials, and get records. Any ten members of the council can suggest projects or changes in rules, and the council president refers these suggestions to the king. The council has a separate budget approved by the king.

The decisions of the Consultative Council are referred to the prime minister who brings them to the Council of Ministers. The Council of Ministers takes care of the executive functions of government, just as a cabinet does in other nations. Most of the ministers are commoners, although members of the royal family hold key positions.

One of the most sensitive areas of the 1992 changes involved the question of the selection of the king. In the past, the crown prince became king on the death of the ruler, and a new crown prince was selected from among the forty or so surviving sons of the kingdom's founder. The new decree abolishes the automatic selection of the crown prince, while confirming the present crown prince as the heir to the throne. It opens up the right to become king to the sons of the founder and the sons of the sons. Now about five hundred princes are eligible, with many of the second generation being young, highly educated, and well traveled. After the reign of the present crown prince, the selection of the king will be through a kind of electoral college of princes of the royal family.

The 1992 decrees also affect local government in the provinces. Governors of the provinces, who report directly to the king, have been given new power in setting priorities on spending and development. New local consultative councils of ten citizens each are to be established for each governor. The governor appoints these local council members in consultation with the interior minister.

The Saudis have a judicial system that involves five types of courts. The system of punishments is based on traditional justice. Death can be the penalty for murder if the victim's relatives choose it rather than financial compensation. Amputation of a hand can be the penalty for stealing, but is rarely used. Stoning can be the penalty for adultery.

The 1992 royal decrees established important guarantees of personal freedoms. Government authorities are prohibited from arresting, spying on, or violating the human rights of citizens without cause. Privacy for telegrams, letters, telephones, and other means of communication are protected. Private homes cannot be entered or searched without legal requirements to do so.

A Saudi soldier

MILITARY

Males between the ages of eighteen and thirty-five are subject to military service. The regular armed forces, consisting of the army, the air force, and a small navy, are under the Ministry of Defense. The police and the coastal and border security forces are under the Ministry of the Interior. The Saudi Arabian National Guard is under the leadership of the crown prince and has the significant role of reinforcing the regular forces in the event of an invasion. However, with an area to defend about the size of the United States east of the Mississippi and with almost no railroad system to move forces and supplies, mobilization of troops to meet an opposing force that could come from a number of directions is no easy matter. The sea and airport facilities have been designed to meet these problems.

The government provides education for these young men (above) in a vocational school and the pupils (left) who attend a girls' elementary school.

EDUCATION

Most schools are run by the government. There are some private schools at the earlier levels of education, but they are small in comparison with government schools.

The few preschools exist primarily in urban areas. Children begin primary education at age six. This phase lasts six years. Intermediate education lasts three years and begins at age twelve. Substantial numbers of children do not continue their education beyond age twelve. Secondary education begins at age fifteen and lasts three years. After the first year in these schools, students go into either a science or an arts program. Specialized schools in commercial, agricultural, technical, and teacher training subjects exist. The government plans to open new schools. Among these will be new schools for the teaching of the Qur'an.

Boys and girls are educated in separate schools. For many years girls were educated at home; there were no schools for them until

*Students can relax at the student center mall
at King Saud University in Riyadh.*

1956. Even today, the traditional role of women leads many families to consider advanced education for females unnecessary and many are concerned about exposing their daughters to modern and foreign values.

Seven universities and sixty-six colleges provide opportunities for higher education for males. There are ten colleges for females.

Adult education is designed to combat illiteracy and to provide follow-up for the education received. The adult courses are for periods of sixteen months. Great gains in education can be seen from the fact that only a couple of generations ago, there was only a 20 percent literacy level in the country, whereas now almost every male child attends primary school.

Handicapped children may attend special schools where they are taught useful skills along with the basic subjects. The government expects these people to be hired so they can lead a useful life.

THE SAUDI FAMILY

The family is the key to Saudi culture, reflecting the desert Bedouin heritage. A family is composed of parents and children plus the other relatives, which includes grandparents, uncles, aunts, and cousins. Marriages are often arranged by families although young people are now more likely to have a role in the choice. Under Islamic law, men may have four wives if they are able to give of their time and material goods equally to each. However, today most men have one wife. Women can write provisions into the marriage contract regarding property disputes, child custody, and divorce. Divorce is easy for the man and not impossible for the woman. However, because the relationship within the family is so important, divorce does not occur that frequently.

The role of women in Saudi society is unusual by Western standards. Interaction with men in public is very restricted. In the cities, women must wear the black veil that covers their clothing and by tradition they do not drive cars. In the sparsely populated countryside, where almost everyone is family, the women go unveiled most of the time and work alongside the men. Although the opportunity for education is recent, Saudi women are eligible for university scholarships. Women are not allowed to attend a lecture given by a male professor, but watching the lecture on closed-circuit television is permitted. Women become physicians, nurses, engineers, social workers, computer operators, and teachers. Some have advanced to administrative positions.

There are many jobs that are not open to women because they would need to work with men, but this is changing slowly. There are exceptions today where women and men work together. With

Most Saudi women are almost completely covered when they appear in public, whether they are shopping in the market (left) or on vacation at the seaside (above).

the increasingly educated female population, more opportunities are likely to open.

Although women cannot travel alone, more and more women, accompanied by their husbands, are traveling abroad. Saudi women carry their own passports with unveiled photographs.

Historically, Muslim women have had more rights than their sisters in the West. Muslim women can inherit and handle their own property. As the wealth of Saudi women has increased with the oil money, so too have the number of women's banks.

Clockwise from above: Fabric and garments for sale in a market in Asir;
a potter making vases and jars on his wheel;
sculptures that show a contemporary version of date palm trees;
and gold jewelry to be worn on the hands

University students performing folk songs

THE ARTS

In the arts, the spoken word has received the greatest honor. Poetry and eloquence are practiced with great skill. The Qur'an forbids the representation of humans and animals, so artists have focused on beautiful abstract designs. These can be found in architecture, textiles, jewelry, and the decoration of weapons and metal utensils. Calligraphy also has been developed to a fine art to embellish the words of the Qur'an and important documents. Because of the Islamic restrictions on subject matter, there is very little visual art, such as painting, photography, or sculpture.

Religion also has affected the literature, because Muhammad did not like the romantic poetry that was popular at the time when he lived. While poetry and storytelling are still important in Arabian life, the subject matter has changed to more factual matters. Now, of course, television, videos, and radio have become popular. Newspapers and magazines also are available.

Most Arabic music is vocal. The Bedouin have a chant that is accompanied by a *rebaba* (a one-stringed instrument) and by drums. With radio and television bringing in other traditions, more music—both traditional Arabic and modern—is heard in the country. Music is not allowed as part of religious services.

73

A boys' gym class being instructed in soccer (above) and entrants in the annual King's Cup Camel Race (left inset)

SPORTS

Soccer is the most popular sport in Saudi Arabia. Group sports, such as soccer, have been cultivated by the Saudis. Although it was not easy to develop this sport in a country that lacks grassy fields and has heat that limits practice time, the national soccer team won the Asia Cup in 1984.

Volleyball, basketball, tennis, and archery are popular. Water sports include swimming, boating, fishing, and scuba diving. The Red Sea is home to many sea creatures that divers find interesting.

The traditional sports of horse and camel racing are still popular. An annual King's Cup Camel Race is held outside Riyadh each year. More than two thousand camels and riders participate. Horse races are held in Riyadh during the winter and

Scuba divers (left) like to dive in the Red Sea. In falconry, a glove protects the falconer from sharp claws and a hood covers the bird's eyes to keep it calm.

spring. Although betting is not permitted, many people attend and cheer on the horses and jockeys.

Although the gun has been banned for hunting in the interests of conservation, hunting with falcons or with saluki hounds is still permitted. Falconry—the capture and training of falcons and hunting with them—requires great skill and takes the participants out into the desert.

CULTURAL CHANGE

The culture of Saudi Arabia has been changing as the country has utilized modern inventions and has sent its youth for study in foreign countries. Change has come slowly, however, and has been weighed against acceptable religious standards.

Ra's at-Tannurah, north of Dammam in the Arabian Gulf, has an oil refinery, liquefied petroleum gas plants, and a marine terminal that handles crude oil and oil and gas products.

Chapter 6

OIL, OIL, AND MORE OIL

The development of the great oil reserves of Saudi Arabia has changed the country from being very poor to being very rich. In many respects, the nation is like a one-industry country because petroleum and petroleum products account for exports greater than all the imports of goods into the country. The boom in the economy has attracted many foreign workers, so that now the work force of 4.8 million is 75 percent from other countries and only 25 percent Saudi. Yemenis, Egyptians, Pakistanis, Koreans, Palestinians, and Filipinos are the major workers, but people from Western countries have also supplied technical expertise.

PETROLEUM

Saudi Arabia is the third-largest producer of petroleum in the world. In 1987, it supplied 7.3 percent of the world output. It is the largest producer within the Organization of Petroleum Exporting Countries (OPEC) and accounts for 22.6 percent of that group's 1987 output. Because of its size, Saudi Arabia has acted as a "swing producer," regulating its production to keep the total output of exports to the OPEC limits. However, the quota system has caused difficulties for the OPEC countries when production has been limited and when the nations cannot agree on appropriate allocations. Still, when OPEC abandoned quotas, the available supply forced the price so low that the group reimposed the production limits.

Decisions about the amount of petroleum to market are not easy because the various producers want to make enough money to meet their national budgets and dreams. Yet too high a price may dry up demand for the product in the long run. Consumers will look for other sources of energy to meet their needs. Another risk is that a high price may unsettle the economies of industrial countries in which the Saudis have investments.

In 1987 Saudi Arabia reported proven reserves of petroleum of 166.6 billion barrels. These reserves would permit ninety more years of production at the 1987 levels. Moreover, new reserves are being discovered as prospectors uncover new fields. In 1987, the nation exported $22.5 billion in petroleum and petroleum products—a figure that can be compared with $20 billion of the country's imports, largely in manufactured goods, transportation equipment, construction materials, and processed food products.

It was 1933 when the Saudis granted a concession to Standard Oil Company of California to explore for oil. That corporation formed the Arabian-American Oil Company (Aramco). By 1946, four oil fields had been discovered and an oil refinery built. Other American firms acquired shares of Aramco, so that in 1948 Standard Oil had 30 percent; Texaco, 30 percent; Exxon, 30 percent; and Mobil, 10 percent. As with other Arab countries, the Saudi government wanted control of its oil industry. In 1973, it took a 25 percent share of Aramco. In 1980, a 100 percent nationalization was agreed on. The Saudi Arabian Oil Company (Saudi Aramco) was formed to take over the nationalized assets. A

An oil pipeline at the port of Yanbu' on the Red Sea

new Supreme Oil Council was established to take charge of the industry. The king chairs the council, which is made up of five private businessmen as well as government ministers to involve the private sector of industry in the management of the business.

Because of the size of the Saudi production, the nation has often been able to affect the world price of petroleum. It has been able to bring prices down by exporting more oil. Since 1984, the nation has bartered its petroleum in exchange for other goods such as aircraft and military equipment.

Most of the Saudi petroleum is shipped by tankers from terminals on the Persian Gulf coast. In 1981 a trans-Arabian pipeline to Yanbu' on the Red Sea was completed, thereby shortening the export route to the United States and Europe. Iraqi oil fields were linked to this Trans-Arabian line in 1985. In 1989, the Saudis announced an eight-hundred-million-dollar plan to build an east-west crude oil pipeline to extend its export capabilities.

Filipino workers at the petrochemical complex at Yanbu'

INDUSTRY

To plan ahead for a time when oil supply or demand may not be as great as now, the Saudis have a goal of encouraging industrial development with the oil money they now are receiving. Refineries and processing plants have been established as joint ventures between the government and foreign countries to take advantage of the immense petroleum and natural gas reserves. Saudi Arabia is the largest producer of petrochemicals in the Middle East and accounts for 5 percent of the world production, according to 1985 figures.

The fertilizer industry is another area that the Saudis are developing. New plants have been built to increase the production of nitrogenous fertilizer, ammonia, urea, sulfuric acid, and melamine.

In the iron and steel industry, new plants help increase production. Manufacture of steel rods and bars, steel billets, and specialized steel wires is being encouraged.

A night view of the industrial section of Yanbu'

Instead of just burning off the natural gas produced by the oil wells, this resource is now being harvested and used as raw material for the petrochemical industry and as an energy source for the steel plants. Facilities to recover sulfur have been established. There have been discoveries and plans for development of gas fields that are not associated with petroleum.

The Saudis encourage private enterprise to develop smaller industries by offering land, credit, and protection with import duties. Building materials such as cement, electrical equipment manufacturing, chemical rubber and plastics production, and food and soft-drink processing have benefited from this policy.

Limestone, gypsum, marble, clay, and salt are now being mined. Deposits of bauxite, iron ore, copper, gold, lead, zinc, silver, and uranium have been discovered and are being studied for development. A gold-mining town was constructed at Mahd adh-Dhahab in 1984.

In 1990 Saudi Arabia announced a fifth five-year development plan that is designed to facilitate growth and diversification of

A large amount of electricity is used every night to light up the city of Jiddah.

industry. The nation spent $776 billion in the first four five-year plans, a total of $65,000 for each of its twelve million citizens.

ELECTRICITY AND WATER

The growth of cities and industry has meant an increase in demand for electrical power. An increasing amount of electricity is now produced in conjunction with seawater desalination.

At first, a large number of small companies were generating the electricity. The government consolidated these by regions, and power is now supplied to each region by a single company. A government corporation responsible for the overall system was formed in 1976 and has been active in establishing power networks in rural areas. The country supplies most of the population with electricity and water.

Water is a special problem. As cities grew, supplying water to the increased population was difficult. Tapping underground water—aquifers (natural underground water supplies) sometimes

Scientists are trying to find the best strain of wheat to grow in the desert.

as deep as 5,577 feet (1,700 meters) — building reservoirs, and constructing dams to catch the runoff of the rainwater are all techniques being used to improve the supply. Desalination of seawater is another important source of fresh water. Saudi Arabia is the world's largest producer of desalinated water. Some of it is carried by pipeline inland to Riyadh and Mecca.

AGRICULTURE AND FISHING

Agriculture amounts to only a small percent of the gross domestic product, although it employs a disproportionately large part of the work force. The labor force involved in agriculture has been declining, even though output has increased. It is possible to grow food only at the oases and irrigated regions — only 1 percent of the total land area. About 39 percent of the land is used for low-grade grazing.

Wheat production has increased greatly. The supply exceeds local demand, so this product can be exported. Production has

*Dates for sale in a market (left) and different kinds of melons (right)
that have been grown on an experimental desert farm.*

been heavily subsidized by the government that paid about six times the average world price for the crop. Subsidies are being withdrawn carefully to provide stability in that segment of the economy and diversification in the country.

Sorghum, barley, and millet also are grown in lesser amounts. Since barley imports jumped, the government has tried to stimulate the production of this crop with subsidies and with the requirement that the six government-owned farms produce more of this crop. Improvement in production will lessen dependence on foreign sources.

At present, Saudi Arabia is the sixth largest exporter of cereal grains. It is the world's largest producer of dates. Watermelons, tomatoes, and grapes also are grown in substantial quantities. By 1986, the country did not need to import eggs or broiler chickens.

A healthy display in a fresh produce market

The greatest problem in the agricultural sector is the scarcity of water. Agriculture accounts for 89 percent of the water needs of the country. Irrigation and other attempts to improve the use of the aquifers will be an important factor in improving production. However, the underground water is being used up at a faster pace than it is being restored by rainwater, so care must be exercised to use this resource wisely. Greater use of desalinated water can be expected to expand the land area that can be cultivated.

Labor is another problem for the Saudis, since people have been moving from rural areas into the cities. Rural facilities are being improved. Capital-intensive, large-scale farming that requires only a small labor force is being encouraged. Dairy production has been started with a strong demand for *laban,* a yogurt drink. Imports of preserved milk are still high.

Left: These fishermen work in the Arabian Gulf.
Right: Some businessmen use the bus for transportation.

Government backing of farmers is also evidenced in interest-free loans and subsidies for fertilizer, farm machinery, and imported breeding stock.

Growth has been recorded in the fishing industry. The 1988 total catch was forty-six thousand tons. About half of the local demand was satisfied by this figure. Certain kinds of fish have been exported to as many as seven countries. New projects include building processing factories and purchasing shrimping vessels. The oil spill in the Persian Gulf harmed the fishing industry. The cleanup of 400 miles (644 kilometers) of gulf waters cost $450 million.

TRANSPORTATION AND COMMUNICATION

The growth of the country can be measured in terms of the development of its transportation facilities. Until 1964 the only

King Fahd Causeway connects Dammam with the island of Bahrain in the Persian Gulf. Saudia airplanes at King Khaled International Airport (inset) in Riyadh

surfaced roads were in the petroleum facilities and in the Jiddah-Mecca-Medina area. Road construction has been a priority since that time. Main and secondary roads have been increased from 4,800 miles to 22,000 miles (7,725 kilometers to 35,405 kilometers).

Seaports and airports with modern facilities also have been constructed. Since 1946 the government has operated Saudia airline. Saudia links local districts in the country as well as providing international flights to destinations in Asia, Europe, Africa, and North America. Railway links are much more limited: a 355-mile (571-kilometer) single-track railroad between Riyadh and Dammam and a 206-mile (322-kilometer) single-track railroad between Riyadh and Hufuf were opened in 1985. A 56-mile (90-kilometer) single-track railway is planned between Jiddah and Mecca to carry pilgrims. A causeway linking neighboring Bahrain to Saudi Arabia was opened in 1986, and plans to build a causeway to Egypt are under discussion.

Although historically, communication improvements were suspect because they could introduce propaganda contrary to Islam, the royal family demonstrated that communications could be used to enhance the teaching of religion. In 1985 Saudi Arabia launched a communications satellite. To make sure everything was correct, payload specialist and astronaut Prince Sultan ibn Salman ibn Abdul Aziz al-Saud accompanied the satellite aboard the U.S. space shuttle *Discovery*.

There are now telephones and radio and television. A number of Arabic newspapers and English-language dailies are published along with periodicals for special interests such as news, women's concerns, and children. However, these are still subject to scrutiny and censorship to bring them into harmony with the demands of the Wahhabi brand of Islam.

TRADE AND FINANCE

Export income—petroleum makes up 90 percent of the value— varies greatly, depending on oil prices and quotas. The main markets for Saudi products are Japan and the United States. These countries also are the chief source of imports.

The Saudis have substantial international reserves. There are twelve commercial banks. Three are wholly owned by the Saudis, and nine are joint ventures. The Saudi Industrial Development Fund (SIDF) provides specialized credit to fund special projects, and there are other institutions that deal with real estate and agriculture. The Saudi Credit Bank provides interest-free loans to low-income Saudis who need money for purposes such as marriage or to make home repairs.

The Saudi Arabian Monetary Agency is charged with responsibility for managing the nation's large foreign assets,

*Left: Financial experts in the dealing room of the
American Bank in Riyadh rely on modern technology for
communication.   Right: The TV tower in Riyadh*

estimated to be $62.3 billion in 1988. Most of this money is held in
banks in the United States and Europe rather than in stocks or real
estate. The nation has been very generous in providing money to
other Islamic states—especially to Iraq during the war with Iran
and to the Palestine Liberation Organization (PLO). Saudi Arabia
also has made loans to countries needing assistance in Africa,
Asia, and Latin America.

HEALTH AND SOCIAL SECURITY

Hospitals have increased during the end of the twentieth
century with a corresponding increase in medical and paramedical
personnel. Health centers and hospitals have the latest technology.

Social security payments are made by the government. All adult
Saudi Arabians, if not independently wealthy, are entitled to a
plot of land and a loan to build a home. In 1988, 347,260 Saudis
received this loan. The government has built housing and has
encouraged private sector building.

Muslim pilgrims—hundreds of thousands of them—travel to Mecca to make the hajj. *They visit the Ka'ba in the Sacred Mosque, which dominates this photograph.*

Chapter 7
THE HAJJ

Mecca in Saudi Arabia is the holiest city of Islam, the second largest religion in the world. It is to Mecca that several million Muslims come each year on a pilgrimage that is called the hajj. It is toward Mecca that Muslims turn to pray wherever they may be in the world. So it is that the word, "Mecca," has come to mean an active place with a great attraction for people.

THE FIVE PILLARS OF ISLAM

Muslims have five duties, called the five pillars of Islam. First, the Muslim must believe and recite the creed, the *shahadah*, "There is no god but God (Allah), and Muhammad is his Prophet." *Allah* is the Arabic word for God, so Muhammad was not introducing a new deity to his people; he was denying the existence of minor gods. *Islam* means "submission to God."

The second duty is daily prayer. At least five times a day, after washing hands, face, and feet, the Muslim faces Mecca and recites specific prayers while following a ritual with the body that involves seven movements, so that the worshiper is sometimes standing and sometimes prostrated with head to the ground.

Third is the giving of money for the needy, called the zakat. It promotes social responsibility by encouraging people to help others who are less fortunate.

The moon is still visible as dawn breaks over the minaret and domes of a mosque in Medina.

Fourth is abstinence during the month of Ramadan, the ninth month in the Muslim calendar. It symbolizes the observance of Muhammad's being given the revelations that were gathered into the Qur'an. While abstaining, from sunrise to sunset Muslims may not eat, drink, smoke, or engage in sexual intercourse. While there are exemptions for people who are infirm and others, abstaining in a desert country such as Saudi Arabia is not easy—especially if the Muslim must engage in physical labor during the day.

Fifth, all Muslims are expected to make the hajj to Mecca at least once in their lifetime if they can afford to do so. There Muslims participate in special rites that are held during the twelfth month of the Islamic lunar calendar.

Muslims usually go to the mosque, a building for worship, on Friday, Islam's holy day. Someone may give a sermon, but there is no priest in the sense of a person who intercedes between God and the worshiper.

The Qur'an

Several branches of Muslims have grown up around different interpretations of the Qur'an and the Sharia, the Islamic law, and around different practices. The Sunnis are the most numerous. The Shi'ites differ in various respects involving their interpretation of the law and the leadership and their customs and festivals. The Wahhabis of Saudi Arabia are Sunnis and are considered very strict in their enforcement of rules regarding dress and abstinence from liquor.

THE ISLAMIC CALENDAR

Most Western nations use the Gregorian calendar, which is based on the 365.242 days it takes for the earth to revolve around the sun. An extra day every fourth year (leap year) uses up the extra time.

The Islamic calendar is based on a lunar year. One lunar month contains 29 days, 12 hours, 44 minutes, and 2.8 seconds. A 12-month year contains 354 days and 11/30 of a day. The fractions add up to 11 days in a cycle of 30 years. During that cycle, an extra day is added to the last month of the year 11 times and creates 11 leap years containing 355 days.

Since each Islamic year begins 10 or 11 days earlier than the previous one, the Islamic calendar is not related to the seasons. Because of this, the same festivals and holidays occur in different seasons in different years.

THE PILGRIM ON THE HAJJ

The pilgrims that stream into Mecca for the hajj use almost every form of transportation. Some Muslims from Africa may walk most of the way. Some from Indonesia may use their life's savings to buy passage on ships to bring them to Saudi Arabia. Most Muslims travel by air to Saudi Arabia.

However different the circumstances of the Muslims making the hajj, they all dress in pilgrim attire. The men wear a two-piece seamless, white, unsewn robe that leaves the right arm and shoulder bare. They wear sandals and go bareheaded. Whether the pilgrim is a king of a country or a laborer, the dress is the same. Women wear a long white robe that covers them from head to foot. The veil or scarf is held off the face. Women may make the pilgrimage unveiled.

Before the pilgrims enter the sacred boundaries of Mecca, they put on these special garments. Mecca is a sanctuary in which no violence is permitted to people, wild animals, or even plants. Only Muslims are permitted to enter. After the pilgrims are dressed appropriately, they are said to be in a state of purity in which they avoid bathing, cutting their hair or nails, violence, arguing, and sexual relations. They declare their desire to obey God by making the hajj. Frequently during the hajj, they cry *"labbayk,"* an ancient Arabic word meaning "I am here!"

RITES OF THE HAJJ

Complicated ceremonies take place during the hajj. During these ceremonies the pilgrims go to places that are significant in the life of Muhammad and earlier prophets. They take place between the eighth and thirteenth days of the twelfth month of the Muslim year. To guide the pilgrims from the many countries through the rituals, guides known as *mutawwifs*, who speak the languages of the pilgrims, are assigned to help them through the performance of the observations. These guides also make the necessary arrangements for the pilgrims' stay in Mecca.

When the pilgrims are properly attired, they may enter the sacred area that Muslims believe was established by Abraham, whom they honor as a prophet along with the other prophets such as Moses, Jesus, and Muhammad. If they have enough time when they first arrive, they will perform the circling of the Ka'ba, drinking water from the sacred Well of Zamzam, and running between the hills of Safa and Marwah.

The Ka'ba is in the center of the Sacred Mosque, a rectangular building of gray stone that is covered with a black cloth. Muslims believe that Abraham dedicated this building to the worship of God and that Muhammad was instructed by God to cleanse the building of the idols that were worshiped there during Muhammad's lifetime.

Pilgrims inside the Holy Mosque in Mecca, with the Ka'ba in the center of the photograph

The Ka'ba is the structure Muslims face when they pray. The black silk covering has verses from the Qur'an inscribed on it in gold and white.

In the east corner of the Ka'ba is a stone about 1 foot (0.3 meter) in diameter that is set in silver. It marks the beginning and end point of the seven trips around the structure. Muslims believe that this black stone is the only part of Abraham's temple that survived. It signifies for them the right hand of God, so they attempt to touch or kiss it as a symbol of their loyalty. Indeed, the sight of the Ka'ba itself can be an intensely emotional experience for Muslims when they first see the object that they face in their prayers.

The Well of Zamzam is sacred, as the well that God showed to Hagar and Ishmael, from whom the Arabs trace their descent. The seven trips between the hills of Safa and Marwah that are now inside the mosque are a reenactment of Hagar's search for water before finding the well. The pilgrims say certain prayers during

Male pilgrims wear a white robe that bares the right arm and shoulder.

this part of the ceremony. The prayers focus on communion with God.

On the eighth day the pilgrims leave Mecca for a short trip of four miles (six kilometers) to Mina, where a tent city is erected to accommodate some of the pilgrims. They spend the night in prayer there, following the example of Muhammad. Then after the dawn prayers, all the pilgrims head for the Plain of Arafat, eight miles (thirteen kilometers) farther east. Cars, buses, trucks, camels, and donkeys are often passed by the walkers because the crush of traffic is so great. The central ritual of the hajj is performed here, as the pilgrims stand and face toward Mecca, praying from noon to sundown. It is here that Muhammad delivered his farewell sermon during his last pilgrimage. The pilgrims are in a sense joining with those who were in the congregation that Muhammad addressed. It is believed that when they leave Arafat they are cleansed of their sins.

After sunset, the pilgrims leave to return to Mecca, stopping for the night at Muzdalifah where they pray and collect pebbles to throw at one of three pillars in Mina that represent Satan. The stoning of Satan represents the pilgrims' resistance to temptation and submission to God and reenacts the response of Ishmael to Satan's temptation of Abraham not to sacrifice his son, Ishmael, according to Islamic tradition.

On the tenth day, each pilgrim buys a goat or sheep and sacrifices it or has a butcher do so in imitation of Abraham's sacrifice to God. The meat is given to the poor. Refrigeration facilities have been built so that the meat will not spoil. This event is paralleled by Muslims throughout the world in the great Islamic festival of the *Id al-Adha*.

With the sacrifice, the major part of the hajj is over. Pilgrims are free to resume their normal dress. As a sign that the restrictions are over, pilgrims clip off a lock of hair or sometimes shave their head.

The pilgrims return to Mecca and repeat the ceremonies that began the hajj by circling the Ka'ba, drinking the water from the well, and going between the hills. Most of the pilgrims return to Mina, where they again stone the pillars. They end their pilgrimage by going to Medina, 200 miles (322 kilometers) north of Mecca, to visit the Prophet's Mosque.

The hajj is a significant event in the life of the pilgrim, who may now carry the title of *haji*. In some places, such as the villages of Egypt, the house of the pilgrim may be painted on the outside with scenes of the pilgrim's journey. Over the centuries, it has required great sacrifices for some to travel to Mecca. Now that so many people can come by air, the title has lost some of the prestige it formerly carried.

CUSTODIANS OF THE HOLY PLACES

To provide for this influx of millions of pilgrims is a huge production. The Ministry of Pilgrimage Affairs and Religious Trusts of the Saudi government is charged with responsibility for handling the logistics and administrative details of the hajj. It works with the Higher Hajj Committee, composed of the amir of Mecca and leaders of that city. However, almost all other departments of the government are involved in dealing with the influx of pilgrims. The hajj becomes the business of the government while the pilgrims are in the country.

The Saudi government is open to criticism from the Muslim world if anything goes wrong. When radicals took over the mosque in Mecca, the Saudis faced a real crisis in dealing with the situation. When some pilgrims were trampled in the air-conditioned tunnel that had been built to assist them, there was an outcry. The establishment of quotas that placed limitations on the number of people able to come to Mecca during the hajj drew great criticism from Iran. That country feared that the Saudis would discriminate against its citizens in setting the limits. While it is a great honor to be responsible for Mecca, it also provides a wealth of problems.

In the past, one of the dangers of making the hajj was contagious disease. Epidemics of smallpox, cholera, and malaria resulted in the death of many pilgrims who were crowded together, often in unsanitary conditions. While it is believed that a person dying on the hajj will go straight to paradise, most pilgrims would prefer to live a while longer. The Saudi government has channeled some of its money into mobile hospitals, portable toilets, disinfectants, and adequate supplies of

King Fahd

pure water. A modern quarantine center at Jiddah has been established. Health conditions now are much improved for the pilgrims.

SAUDIS AND THE FUTURE

In many ways the role of the Saudis in the hajj symbolizes the history of the country. Ibn Saud took Mecca by force of arms, and his family rules the country he consolidated with absolute power. They are proud to be Arabs, to be from the land where Muhammad received the revelations that make up the Qur'an, to be of the tribe that God has blessed with the wealth of oil. Just as

Saudi Arabian portraits clockwise from above left: a
street vendor, a pediatrician, and two young students

A typical open-air market

Mecca is off-limits to non-Muslims, so the country tries to minimize foreign influences that would disturb their traditional culture. Yet the Saudis have used modern inventions to further that culture and to protect the pilgrims on the hajj.

Saudi Arabia will be challenged to use its wealth wisely to develop its human resources and its economic base. Other Arab nations may be jealous of its oil riches. The wealth gives the Saudis power on the world scene to help protect or disrupt the economic stability of the West. Saudi Arabia has come far in learning how to use its power. There remains the difficulty of balancing individual rights and responsibilities as a world power with the customs that were developed in a desert tribal setting.

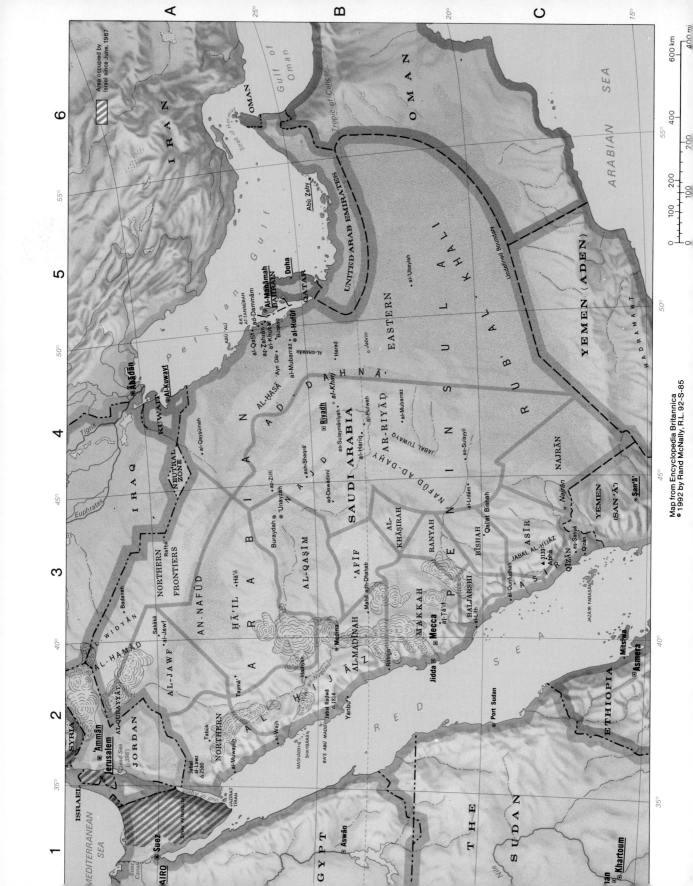

Map from Encyclopedia Britannica
© 1992 by Rand McNally, R.L. 92-S-85

MAP KEY

If the place name is spelled differently in the text, it appears in parenthesis after the name that appears on the map.

Place	Grid
Abha	C3
Abu Madd, Ra's, *point*	B2
Abu' Ali, *island*	A4
ad-Dahna', (Dahna'), *desert*	A4, B4
ad-Dammam, (Dammam)	A5
ad-Dawadimi	B3
'Afif, *province*	B3
al-Ghawar, *hills*	A4, B4
al-Hamad, *plain*	A2
al-Hariq	B4
al-Hasa, (Hasa), *region*	A4
al-Hijaz, (Hijaz), *region*	A2, B2
al-Hufuf, (Hufuf)	A4
al-Hulwah	B4
al-Jawf	A2
al-Jawf, *province*	A2, A3
al-Kharj, *oasis*	B4
al-Khasirah, *province*	B3
al-Khubar, (Khubar)	A4
al-Lidam	B3
al-Lith	B3
al-Madinah, (Madinah), *province*	B2, B3
al-Mubarraz	A4
al-Mubarraz	B4
al-Muwaylih	A2
al-Qasim, *province*	A3, B3
al-Qatif	A4
al-Qaysumah	A4
al-Qunfudhah	C3
al-Qurayyat, *province*	A1
al-'Ubaylah	B5
al-Wajh	A2
al-Widyan, *plateau*	A2, A3
an-Nafud, *desert*	A3
ar-Riyad, *province*	A3, A4, B3, B4, C3, C4
as-Sabya, (Sabya)	C3
as-Sulaymaniyah	B4
ash-Shaqra'	B4
Asir, *province*	A4
Asir, *region*	C3
at-Ta'if, (Ta'if)	B3
'Ayn Dar	A4
az-Zahran	A5
az-Zilfi	A3
Badanah	A3
Baljarishi, *province*	B4
Bishah, *province*	B3
Buqayq	A4
Buraydah	A3
Dahy, Nafud ad, *desert*	B3, B4
Eastern, *province*	C4, B4, B5, B6
Farasan, Jaza'ir, *islands*	C3
Hadiyah	A2
Ha'il	A3
Ha'il, *province*	A2
Harad	A2, A3
Hijaz, Jabal al-, (Hijaz), *mountains*	B4
Jabrin, *oasis*	C3
Jidda, (Jiddah)	B4
Lawz, Jabal al-, *mountain*	B2
Mahd adh-Dhahab	B3
Mecca, *province*	B2, B3
Mashabih, *island*	A2
Mecca	B2
Medina	B2
Najd, *region*	A3, A4, B4
Najran, *oasis*	C3
Najran, *province*	C3, C4
Northern, *province*	A3
Northern Frontiers, *province*	A2
Nuqumi, Wadi an-, *watercourse*	A3
Persian Gulf	A2, B2
Qal'at Bishah	A4, A5, B5
Qizan	C3
Qizan, *province*	C3
Rabigh	B2
Radwa, Jabal, *mountain*	B2
Rafha'	A3
Ranyah, *province*	B3
Red Sea	A1, A2, B2, C2, C3
Riyadh	B4
Rub' al-Khali, *desert*	B5, C4, C5
Sakaka	A3
Shaybara, *island*	A2
Tabuk	A2
Tannurah, Ra's at-, *cape*	A5
Tayma, (Tayma')	A2
Tiran, Jazirat, *island*	A1
Tuwayq, Jabal, *mountains*	B4
'Unayzah	A3
Yanbu'	B2

A carpet vendor in Medina

MINI-FACTS AT A GLANCE

GENERAL INFORMATION

Official Name: Al-Mamlakah al-Arabiyah as-Saudiyah (The Kingdom of Saudi Arabia)

Capital: Riyadh

Government: The authority of the king is based on Islamic law (*Sharia*). The king is the head of state and the government. Religious leaders play an important role in the running of the government. The holy book, the Qur'an, is the constitution; there is no other written constitution, no political parties, and no national elections. Judges are independent and governed by the rule of Islamic laws. The kingdom is divided into four regions (Central, Eastern, Southwest, and Western) and 14 administrative districts.

In 1992 King Fahd issued a royal decree called the "Basic System of Government." This decree promotes decentralization of power and establishes a bill of rights for the first time. It also abolishes the automatic selection of the crown prince.

Religion: Islam is the official religion. Friday is the holy day of the week when people attend noon prayers in the mosques. The overwhelming majority of Saudi Arabians are Muslims who follow Islam. Almost 85 percent are Sunni Muslims; Shi'ites live mainly in the Eastern Province. Saudi Arabia is the birthplace of the Prophet Muhammad and the home of Islam's two most important shrines — Mecca and Medina. The Qur'an is the basis of daily life and traditions. People following other faiths account for less than 2 percent (mostly foreigners) of the total population.

Millions of Muslim pilgrims visit Mecca and Medina each year. The Ministry of Pilgrimage Affairs and Religious Trusts handles the administrative details of the *hajj* — the religious journey. Non-Muslims are forbidden to enter Mecca.

Ethnic Composition: Saudis of Arab origin form the largest ethnic group (82 percent), followed by Yemeni Arabs (10 percent), other Arabs (3 percent), and others (5 percent). Some Turks, Iranians, Indonesians, Indians, and Africans who came as Muslim pilgrims reside in the Hijaz region. There is a large number of expatriate workers and technical experts from Egypt, Europe, Korea, North America, Pakistan, Palestine, the Philippines, and Yemen.

Language: Arabic is the official language. Arabic is also the language of the Qur'an. English is taught in secondary schools and is used in educated circles and business.

National Flag: The traditional Wahhabi banner is the Saudi state flag. Officially adopted in 1973, the green and white flag displays the word of the Unity of Islam "There is no God but God; Muhammad is the messenger of God" in Arabic script. Beneath the script is a white sword—a symbol of Islamic justice and righteousness. The inscription is sewn in such a way so it reads correctly on both sides. The flag of Saudi Arabia is never flown half-staffed for any reason.

National Emblem: The national emblem is two gold-hilted silver swords crossed below the base of a tall palm tree; the palm tree represents patience and endurance.

National Anthem: The Royal anthem is an instrumental piece without words.

National Calendar: The Islamic calendar is based on a lunar year of 354 days. The Muslim day begins at sunset and is divided into two 12-hour periods.

Money: The Saudi riyal (SR) is divided into 100 halalah. In 1992, 1 Saudi riyal was equal to $0.26 in U.S. currency.

Membership in International Organization: Arab League, Gulf Cooperation Council (GCC); International Monetary Fund (IMF); Islamic Development Bank; Organization of Petroleum Exporting Countries (OPEC), United Nations

Weights and Measures: The metric system is in use.

Population: 14,691,000 (1991 estimates); more than one-third of the population is of resident foreigners; seventy-seven percent urban and 23 percent rural. Density is rather low with just 17 persons per sq. mi. (six persons per sq km). Some oases have densities of 2,000 persons per sq. mi. (770 persons per sq km).

Cities:

Jiddah	1,300,000
Riyadh	1,000,000
Mecca	550,000

```
Ta'if. . . . . . . . . . . . . . . . . . . . . . . . . . . . . . . . . . . . . . . . . . . . . . . . . . .   300,000
Medina. . . . . . . . . . . . . . . . . . . . . . . . . . . . . . . . . . . . . . . . . . . . . . . .   290,000
Dammam. . . . . . . . . . . . . . . . . . . . . . . . . . . . . . . . . . . . . . . . . . . . . .   200,000
```
(Population figures based on 1980 estimates.)

GEOGRAPHY

Border: Seven countries share international borders with Saudi Arabia—Jordan, Iraq, Kuwait, Qatar, United Arab Emirates, Oman, and Yemen. Only a few of the boundaries have been precisely measured and determined. The Red Sea and the Gulf of Aqaba make the western boundary.

Coastline: 1,515 mi. (2,438 km)

Land: Saudi Arabia comprises about four-fifths of the Arabian Peninsula and is the third-largest country in Asia after China and India. Some one-third of the total area is sandy desert, including the Rub al-Khali (Empty Quarter). *An-Nafud*, "the Great Nafud" sand desert is located in the interior. A narrow coastal plain stretches along the Red Sea. The land slopes from the rugged mountains in the southwest toward the Persian Gulf in the east.

Major regions are the Hijaz along the Red Sea coast, the Asir mountainous region in the southwest, the central heartland of Najd where Riyadh is located, the Hasa or the Eastern Province containing the world's largest deposits of proven oil reserves, and the northern region with a large concentration of nomads.

Highest Point: 10,279 ft. (3,133 m) in the Asir region

Lowest Point: Sea level

Rivers: Saudi Arabia has no permanent rivers or bodies of water. Some seasonal riverbeds (*wadis*) exist. Underground water tapped by wells is of vital importance.

Forests: Because of aridity and salinity, vegetation is sparse. Just a little over 0.5 percent of land is under forests and shrubs. Meadows and pastures cover some 40 percent of the land. Frankincense and myrrh were the two most important gum resin products of Arabia in historical times. Date palm, mangrove, juniper, tamarisk, and acacia are common. The date palm's trunk, branches, and fiber are used for different purposes. The Asir National Park in the east was created to preserve the landforms, flora, and animal life of the Asir region.

Wildlife: Wild animals include the oryx, ibex, gazelle, jerboa, fox, lynx, rabbit, hedgehog, sand cat, gerbil, baboon, hyena, wolf, panther, and jackal. Bustard is the favorite game bird; eagles, vultures, owls, flamingoes, egrets, swallows, and cuckoos are found mostly in the coastal areas. Sand grouse and larks inhabit desert regions. Arabian horses are world renowned for sports purposes. Scorpions, lizards, and snakes are numerous. White donkeys and camels are domesticated. The camel's traditional importance to desert life can be measured by its nickname "ship of the desert."

Climate: Saudi Arabia is one of the hottest regions in the world. In the interior, average summer temperatures are 112° F (44.4° C). Rainfall is very little and erratic, averaging some 4 in. (10 cm) a year except in the Asir region where 12 to 30 in. (30 to 75 cm) of rain falls in the summer. Frost and freezing temperatures are common in winter. Severe dust storms occur in the summer.

Greatest Distance: North to South: 1,145 mi. (1,843 km)
East to West: 1,290 mi. (2,076 km)

Area: 830,000 sq. mi. (2,149,690 sq km)

ECONOMY AND INDUSTRY

Agriculture: Less than 1 percent of Saudi Arabia is under cultivation. The chief agricultural products are wheat, watermelons, dates, barley, tomatoes, sorghum, grapes, cucumbers, gherkins, pumpkins, squash, gourds, eggplants, carrots, potatoes, indigo, onions, and pulses (beans). Alfalfa—a fodder for livestock—can be grown among date palms in oases. Some cotton is also produced. Coffee is cultivated on the mountain slopes in the Asir region and roses are grown on acres of land near Ta'if. In the Asir region, cultivation is extended by irrigation from the Jizan Dam.

Some 40 percent of the land is used for grazing. Sheep, goats, camels, and cattle are the chief livestock. The camel is not only useful for transportation, it gives milk and meat for human consumption, its hair is used for clothing, and its dung provides fuel for fires. Sheep are kept for their meat and wool and goats for goat cheese. There is a small fishing industry along the coasts.

Mining: Some of the largest petroleum deposits in the world are found in Saudi Arabia. Proven oil reserves are estimated at more than 167 billion barrels, about one-fifth of the world's proven reserves. Gypsum, limestone, marble, clay, and salt are mined. Some deposits of bauxite, iron ore, copper, gold, lead, zinc, silver, and uranium have been recently discovered. In 1989 some 1,834,683,000 barrels of oil and 26,708,000,000 cubic meters of natural gas were produced.

Manufacturing: Saudi Arabia has few manufacturing industries. The fertilizer industry is being expanded. Other manufacturing industries are cement, electrical equipment, rubber and plastic products, food and soft drink processing, steel rods and bars, and petrochemicals such as methanol, ethylene, urea, ethylene glycol, ethanol, and caustic soda. Saudi Arabia is the world's largest producer of desalinated water.

Transportation: All major towns are connected with good all-weather roads. There are some 22,000 mi. (7,725 km) of roads but railway links are limited. The national airline is Saudia. King Abd al-Aziz International Airport in Jiddah is basically used by pilgrims coming to the holy towns of Mecca and Medina. King Fahd International Airport at Riyadh connects Saudi Arabia with most of the world. There are some 25 airports with scheduled flights. A new airport opened at Jubail in 1986. The chief seaport is Jiddah, followed by Dammam, Yanbu', Gizan, Jubail, and an oil port at Ras Tanura. There were some 2,300,000 cars in the late 1980s.

Communication: The Ministry of Communication regulates postal, telephone, cable, and wireless services. The first newspaper, *al-Oiblah*, was found in 1915. Newspapers are privately owned; criticism of Islam and the royal family is not permitted. There are some 10 daily newspapers; the press is subject to government censorship. In the early 1990s there were 3.5 persons for each radio and television and 13 persons per one telephone.

Trade: Saudi Arabia is the world's leading oil exporter. Oil accounts for nearly 90 percent of the country's total exports. Throughout the 1980s, Saudi Arabia had a trade surplus (more exports than imports). The chief imports are transport equipment, machinery and appliances, foodstuffs, textiles and clothing, metal articles, and chemicals. The United States, Japan, United Kingdom, Germany, Italy, Switzerland, France, and South Korea are the main import sources.

The major exports are petroleum (both crude and refined) and petroleum products. The chief export destinations are the United States, Japan, Singapore, France, Bahrain, The Netherlands, and Italy.

EVERYDAY LIFE

Health: Hospitals and medical personnel have increased significantly in recent years. In the early 1990s there were some 850 people per doctor and about 250 persons per hospital bed—a ratio similar to that in the United States. The major diseases are cholera, meningitis, yellow fever, typhoid, tuberculosis, lung infections, and asphyxia. The King Faisal Medical City near Riyadh is probably the most technically advanced hospital complex in the world. The Jiddah Quarantine Center for some 2,400 pilgrim patients is designed by the World Health Organization (WHO). Life expectancy at birth is 62 years for males and 65 years for females.

Education: Education is not compulsory, but is free of charge, including university education. Primary education begins at age six and lasts six years. Three years of intermediate education begins at age 12. Secondary education of three years begins at age 15. There are 7 universities and 66 colleges for men, and 10 colleges and one institution of higher learning for women. Some 30 special institutes provide education for handicapped children. Men and women attend separate schools and universities. In 1990, the literacy rate was about 63 percent. Vocational training is encouraged to lower dependence on foreign workers; there are some 30 vocational centers. Specialized engineering training is provided at the University of Petroleum and Minerals at Dahran and Sharia law studies are provided at the Islamic University at Medina. Some 4 to 5 thousand Saudi students study in the United States.

Official Holidays:
National Day
Unification of the Kingdom Day

All of the Islamic holidays are based on the lunar calendar and they vary by a few days every year. The major Muslim holidays are Id al-Adha (Feast of Sacrifice), Id al-Fitr (the end of Ramadan), Mawlud (Birth of the Prophet), Laylat al-Mi'raj (Ascension of the Prophet), 1st of Muharram (Muslim New Year), and Ashura (10th of Muharram).

Culture: Since the Islamic religion discourages the representation of humans and animals, artists have focused on beautiful abstract designs. There is very little visual art such as painting, photography, or sculpture. Graphic and Islamic art (calligraphy) is officially encouraged. Saudi law does not permit men and women to attend public events together; they are segregated in their work place also. Women are not allowed to drive cars or bicycles and cannot travel alone. The work week extends from Saturday to Wednesday with Thursday and Friday being the weekend. The majority of the Saudi Arabians wear traditional Arab dress; men wear a white flowing robe (*thawb*) and a head cloth (*ghutrah*), women wear a black robe over their clothes called an *aba* and frequently cover their faces with veils.

The King Faisal Award annually recognizes works in humanitarian and scientific fields. Music is not allowed as a part of Islamic religious services. King Saud University Library system is the largest with more than 1,000,000 volumes. The Museum of Archaeology and Ethnography is at Riyadh.

Family: Families in general are extended and live together in one house. Marriages often are arranged by families. A traditional Saudi wedding is an Islamic civil ceremony; men pay dowries for their brides. Islamic law allows a man to have up to 4 wives, although that is not common. Divorce does not occur frequently.

Housing: The government has encouraged nomadic tribes to settle in the cities and has subsidized housing projects with oil revenues. The government provides land and about $90,000 in no-interest loans to any Saudi Arabian desiring to build a house. The capital city of Riyadh was a walled town built with mud bricks in the 1940s. High-rise apartment buildings have largely replaced these small mud houses, but apartments are in short supply. Some Bedouin still are nomads and live near oases in large tents made of animal wool. Most Bedouin have given up their tents for houses and their camels for trucks. The oil money has significantly improved the standard of living in Saudi Arabia.

Food: With less than 1 percent of the area under cultivation, Saudi Arabia must import most of its food. A Saudi meal consists of rice with mildly spiced lamb or chicken, dates, and dairy products. Lamb served on a bed of seasoned rice is a usual dish. Pork products are forbidden. Food is traditionally eaten with the hands while sitting cross-legged on the floor. Tea or coffee is served at all meetings. Buttermilk, camel's milk, *laban*, a yogurt drink, and cola are also popular beverages. Banquets are served on rugs. *Arikah* is a special bread that is broken off and fashioned into the shape of a spoon to be dipped into a side dish of honey. Sale or use of alcohol is prohibited by Saudi law. Anyone with possession of harmful drugs may face the death penalty. Smoking is not encouraged. During the month of Ramadan, the ninth month of the Muslim calendar, all Muslims must abstain from food and liquids during the daylight hours.

Sports and Recreation: Soccer is the national sport. Volleyball, basketball, tennis, and archery also are popular. The use of guns for hunting has been banned. Traditional sports include hunting with saluki hounds, falconry, and horse and camel racing. An annual King's Cup Camel Race is held outside Riyadh each year. The Riyadh Stadium is complete with Olympic size running tracks and soccer fields.

Social Welfare: Medical assistance is free for all Saudi citizens, foreign residents, and pilgrims. The Social Security Administration provides for the needy people. All adult Saudi Arabians are entitled to a plot of land and a loan in order to build a home.

IMPORTANT DATES

4000 to 2000 B.C.—Dilmun civilization flourishes in Arabian Peninsula

A.D. 70—Fall of Jerusalem to Rome

c. 570—The Prophet Muhammad is born in Mecca; an Abyssinian protectorate is established in the Arabian Peninsula

610—The Prophet Muhammad reports about his revelations from the angel Gabriel

622—Muhammad and his followers move to Medina (the *Hijra*); beginning of the Muslim calendar

627—Battle of the Ditch

630—Muhammad, with a ten-thousand-strong armed force, conquers Mecca

632—Muhammad dies

711-715—Muslims move into Spain

750—Baghdad (Iraq) becomes the center of Islamic power

1238—Muslims build the Alhambra in Granada, Spain

1248—Christian Crusaders fight and defeat the Muslims in Seville, Spain

Mid-1400s—The Saudi family establishes control over Diriyah

1516-17—The Ottoman Turks establish rule in Egypt and Syria

1669—Ottomans are driven out of the eastern coast of the Arabian Peninsula

1750—The first Saudi state is formed under a local ruler, Muhammad ibn Saud

Mid-1700—The Wahhabi movement spreads across most of Arabia

1765—Most of the Najd become Wahhabis through efforts of Muhammad ibn Saud, ruler of the oasis of Dirivah, and Abd al-Wahhabi

1792—Abd al-Wahhabi dies

1801—Karbala, a Shi'ite holy city, is attacked; Wahhabis take over Mecca

1805—Wahhabis take over Medina

1814—Ottoman troops occupy the Hijaz region

1818—Ottomans occupy the Najd region and capture the capital city of Diriyah

1824—The capital is established at Riyadh by the Saud family

1828—Faisal, son of Turki ibn Abd Allah, escapes from Egyptian prison

1834—Faisal becomes king

1865—Faisal dies

1891—Tribal chiefs and Ottoman Turks gain control over most of Arabia; Abd al-Rahman is forced out of Riyadh with his family, takes shelter in Kuwait

1902—Ibn Saud, son of Abd al-Rahman, captures Riyadh from the rival al-Rashid family

1913-26—Najd, Hasa, and Hijaz regions are conquered by Ibn Saud

1915—*Al-Qiblah* newspaper is founded

1916 — All Bedouin tribes are ordered to join the *Ikhwan*, "brothers or brethren"

1925 — The Sharif rule ends in the Hijaz

1926 — The first public schools for boys are established

1927 — Treaty of Jiddah establishes Saudi authority from the Persian Gulf to the Red Sea

1929 — A pan-Islamic Conference is held in Mecca; Battle of Sibila

1932 — Kingdom of Saudi Arabia is proclaimed; Ibn Saud becomes king

1933 — The Saudi Arabian petroleum industry is established

1934 — The boundary with Yemen is determined

1938 — The first large-scale deposit of oil is discovered

1944 — The Arabian American Oil Company (Aramco) is founded; oil revenues exceed 4 million dollars

1945 — Saudi Arabia joins the Arab League

1946 — The government starts operating Saudia Airlines

1948 — The state of Israel is established

1951 — Saudi Arabia grants the United States usage rights at the Dahran airfield

1953 — King Ibn Saud dies; he is succeeded by his son Abd al-Aziz al-Saud

1954 — Saudi Arabia signs the Convention for the Prevention of Pollution of the Sea by Oil

1956 — Diplomatic relations are broken with the United Kingdom and France after Britain, France, and Israel invade Egypt; first public school for girls is opened

1957 — University of Riyadh is founded

1960—Saudi Arabia becomes a founding member of Organization of Petroleum Exporting Countries (OPEC)

1961—University of Medina is founded

1962—Slavery is officially abolished; the Red Crescent Society is founded; Dahran Air Base is closed; under a broad reform program the Social Security Administration is established

1963—Ties with the United Kingdom are resumed

1964—King Saud is deposed and replaced as king by King Faisal

1965—Saudi television starts transmission

1967—Abd al-Aziz University is founded in Jiddah; Trans-Arabian highway is completed; Saudi Arabia supports Egypt, Jordan, and Syria in the Six-Day War against Israel

1968—The National Library is founded in Riyadh

1969—Islamic summit meeting is held in Rabat, Morocco

1971—The Saudi-Kuwaiti neutral zone is partitioned for administrative purposes

1973—In support of the Arab cause during the Arab-Israel war, Saudi Arabia joins in the Arab oil boycott of the United States; the current flag is officially adopted

1974—Dispute over Buraymi Oasis is settled with the United Arab Emirates

1975—King Faisal is assassinated; he is succeeded by his brother, Khalid

1978—The Museum of Archaeology and Ethnography is opened at Riyadh; legislation forbids the felling of trees; United States President Carter announces sale of 60 F15 fighter bombers to Saudi Arabia

1979—The Grand Mosque at Mecca is taken over by a radical group of 250 people; it is taken back after two weeks of fighting

1980—100 percent nationalization of Aramco is agreed upon

1981—King Abd al-Aziz International Airport is opened; a trans-Arabian pipeline is completed

1982—King Khalid dies; he is succeeded by Prince Fahd; Asir National Park is established

1983—King Fahd International Airport is opened

1984—The national soccer team wins the Asia Cup; a gold-mining town is constructed at Mahd al-Dhahab

1985—Oil production drops to 2 million barrels a day; King Fahd visits the United States; Saudi Arabia launches a communication satellite

1986—King Fahd revives the title of Custodian of the Two Holy Mosques; a causeway linking Saudi Arabia with Bahrain is opened; Saudi Arabia becomes self-sufficient in the production of eggs and broiler chickens

1987—Diplomatic ties with Egypt are reestablished; armed clashes occur between Iranian pilgrims and the Saudi forces in Mecca killing 402 people; Saudi Arabia supplies 7.3 percent of the world petroleum output

1988—King Fahd plays an important role in bringing about cease-fire between Iran and Iraq; country's foreign assets are estimated at $62,300 million

1990—Iraq invades Kuwait; 27 countries form a coalition against Iraq and move into the eastern part of Saudi Arabia at the invitation of the Saudi rulers to protect their borders; some 50 women automobile drivers stage a protest against the Saudi ban on female drivers; the women are promptly threatened with an unspecified punishment; some 1,400 pilgrims die in a stampede in an air-conditioned tunnel in Mecca

1991—Iraq breaks diplomatic relations with Saudi Arabia; Kuwait's crown prince and government in exile take refuge in Saudi Arabia

1992—King Fahd issues a series of decrees aimed at decentralizing political power and protecting certain individual rights; an attempt is made to codify Saudi law in a written constitution

IMPORTANT PEOPLE

Abd al-Aziz ibn Abd al-Rahman al-Faisal al-Saud (1881-1952), known as Ibn Saud; established the present Kingdom of Saudi Arabia in 1902; ruled from 1932 to 1953

Abd al-Rahman, father of Ibn Saud; the last ruler to use *imam*, a religious title

Abu Bakr, the compromise candidate as Muhammad's successor; reigned from 632 to 634; the rightful successor of Muhammad according to the Sunnis

Ali, Prophet Muhammad's cousin, foster brother, and son-in-law; Fatima's husband; the rightful successor of Muhammad according to the Shi'ites; reigned as caliph from 656 to 661

Fahd ibn Abd al-Aziz Al Saud (1921-   ), head of state and prime minister of Saudi Arabia since 1982

Faisal ibn Abd al-Aziz Al Saud (1906-75), credited with transforming Saudi Arabia into one of the most stable and influential countries of the Middle East; ruled from 1964 to 1975

Fatima (c.616-33), Prophet Muhammad's daughter and Ali's wife

Sharif Ghalib, administrator of Mecca and Medina in the early 1800s

Hussein, a Hashemite Sharif of Mecca backed by the Ottomans

Hussein, Saddam (1937-   ), dictator of Iraq; invaded Kuwait in 1990

Ibn Saud (1880-1953), also known as Abd al-Aziz ibn Abd al-Rahman al-Faisal al-Saud, the father of contemporary Saudi Arabia

Khadija, wife of Prophet Muhammad

Khalid ibn Abd al-Aziz (1913-82), half-brother of King Faisal; king and prime minister from 1975 to 1982

Khalid ibn al-Walid, a general known as the "Sword of God"

Khomeini, Ayatollah (1903-89), militant Shi'ite leader of Iran

Lawrence, T.E. (1888-1935), also known as Lawrence of Arabia; British archaeological scholar and military strategist

Muhammad (c.570-632), prophet of Islam

Muhammad Ali, Ottoman viceroy in Cairo

Muhammad ibn Rashid, an administrator in Najd region

Muhammad ibn Saud, ruler of the oasis of Diriyah

Saud ibn Abd al-Aziz, king of Saudi Arabia, ruled from 1953 to 1964

Sheikh Muhammad ibn Abd al-Wahhab (1703?-91), a scholar and a
fundamentalist reformer; started the Wahhabi movement

Prince Sultan ibn Salman ibn Abd al-Aziz, an astronaut who helped launch a
communication satellite aboard the U.S. space shuttle *Discovery*

Turki ibn Abd Allah (?-1834), drove Egyptians out of Najd

Ahmad Zaki Yamani (1930-   ), former minister of petroleum and mineral
resources; known as spokesman for the oil-exporting countries

Compiled by Chandrika Kaul

The emblem of the kingdom of Saudi Arabia

A children's playground in the town of Abha

INDEX

Page numbers that appear in boldface type indicate illustrations

About the Author

Leila Merrell Foster is a lawyer, United Methodist minister, and clinical psychologist with degrees from Northwestern University and Garrett Evangelical Theological Seminary. She is the author of books and articles on a variety of subjects.

Dr. Foster's love of travel began early as she listened to her mother and older sister read travel and adventure stories. As a youngster, she enjoyed the family trips through which she learned geography, geology, history, art, agriculture, and economics in a very pleasant manner.

Dr. Foster also has written Enchantment of the World: *Bhutan, Iraq, Lebanon,* and *Jordan.*